Saratoga Stories

Saratoga Stories

Gangsters, Gamblers & Racing Legends

Jon Bartels

LEXINGTON, KENTUCKY

EP
ECLIPSE
PRESS

Library of Congress Cataloging-in-Publication Data

Bartels, Jon, 1951 –
    Saratoga stories : gangsters, gamblers, and racing legends / by Jon Bartels.
        p. cm.
    Includes bibliographical references.
    ISBN 978-1-58150-158-2 (hardcover)
1.   Saratoga Racecourse (Saratoga Springs, N.Y.)- -History. 2. Horse
Racing- -New York (State)- -Saratoga Springs- -History. 3. Race horses- -United
States- -History.   I. Title.
  SF335.U6N668   2007
  798.4006'874748 - - dc22
. . . .   2007011646

Printed in the United States
First Edition: 2007

a division of
Blood-Horse Publications
PUBLISHERS SINCE 1916

CONTENTS

Introduction

Long before there was Las Vegas, there was Saratoga. In a time before radio and television, Americans in the Gilded Age viewed Saratoga Springs as the culmination of their hopes and dreams. In this picturesque resort town in upstate New York, captains of industry and the very wealthy mingled with middle-class visitors every summer during a six-week period punctuated by social events, parties, business, and, of course, the races. Saratoga Race Course was the showcase of American horse racing, bringing in thousands of visitors eager to experience the glitz and glamour of "the Season."

Not much has changed in Saratoga since the late nineteenth century — at least as far as the racing scene goes. Captains of industry still mingle with the middle class in the expansive Saratoga paddock; parties and galas fill the social calendar. While most of the grand hotels along Main Street are long gone, the many smaller hotels and bed and breakfasts have been long booked before the race meet begins.

For many reasons Saratoga remains an important part of Americana: the social life; a stroll down Union Avenue from the track to Congress Park to admire the brilliant flower beds and the splendid Victorian architecture; tickets for a summer show of the New York City Ballet or Philadelphia Orchestra; a walk among the writers, artists, and musicians who congregate at Yaddo; a visit to the site of the Battle of Saratoga Springs, where the British surrendered to the Continental Army; the saline spring water; a drive to nearby Lake George for hiking and water sports; or the chance to discover the next Man o' War, who was purchased at the prestigious Saratoga yearling sale in 1918.

While these are all compelling reasons to visit Saratoga, the main attraction has always been to see world-class Thoroughbreds run. Ever since Stephen Foster immortalized one of Saratoga's first champions with the popular song "The Old Grey Mare, She Ain't What She Used to Be," late summer has been a showcase for Saratoga: great races and great horses.

With Saratoga's contemporary prominence, it is almost too easy to dismiss the noteworthy individuals and circumstances that led to Saratoga's pride of place in the racing world. Barely weeks after the smoke had cleared from the blood-drenched fields of Gettysburg, Pennsylvania, where two cultures collided, the first races at Saratoga attracted America's finest racehorses on a track built under the guidance of John Morrissey.

Morrissey could not have been a more unlikely founder. A self-confessed former chicken thief, street thug, and criminal, he was also an immensely successful gambler with a vision to bring Thoroughbred racing to Saratoga.

Despite Morrissey's less-than-exemplary past, with the support of men such as Cornelius Vanderbilt, John R. Hunter, Leonard Jerome, William Travers, and Jay Gould, he gained the social and professional backing to be accepted as a business leader in Saratoga. With their help, Morrissey not only established Saratoga as a leading racetrack but also guided Saratoga to the pinnacle of prestige in America's Gilded Age.

The early nineteenth century was a time of expansion led

by clever and sometimes ruthless entrepreneurs who seized opportunity and created industries that dominated the economy. With the rapid growth of the railroads, the boundaries of the new nation and its economy expanded. Rapid economic growth allowed laborers to migrate easily and more cheaply to frontier areas for settlement. It also made accessible the vast natural wealth of the land. Later in the century, falling prices, increased wages, and the creation of disposable income for households across the country were instrumental to the development of resorts such as Saratoga. The first of the Morrissey's race meetings drew horses from at least four states (Kentucky, Missouri, New Jersey, and New York) and Canada and represented at least fourteen stables. The years, however, have clouded memories of just how difficult it was for Morrissey and his backers to establish a tradition of excellence. In 1863, the first year of Thoroughbred racing at Saratoga, the meeting was marred by an attempt to drug one of the season's leading horses; the next season was tainted by the appearance of a soon-to-be notorious character and a scandal that engulfed one of the leading horses of the season.

Despite the rocky beginning, the meetings have continued for almost 150 years, providing a showcase for the top Thoroughbreds in the country. For more than a century, fans have filled the stands to watch top racehorses such as Colin and Man o' War compete.

Another link to the past is the legacy of the sensational upsets at Saratoga, often called the "graveyard of champions." The names of the heavily favored casualties that came to Saratoga but lost include some of the finest Thoroughbreds ever to grace American tracks, including Duke of Magenta, Hindoo, and Man o' War.

The great races and the upsets must be seen for what they actually were: the result of keen competition among very strong, fast, and often courageous athletes. The memories of these races continue to beckon future generations. Since those first races in 1863, almost magical performances resonating with the mystical bond that links horse and man have delighted Saratoga's crowds.

CHAPTER 1

John Morrissey:
A Vision and a Beginning

A more unlikely candidate to found America's most revered and storied racetrack could not have been imagined. John Morrissey was born in Templemore, County Tipperary, Ireland, on February 12, 1831. Two years later the Morrissey family immigrated to New York City, then moved to Troy, a small town near Albany in upstate New York.

His father, Timothy Morrissey, was a common laborer with little education. John went to school for one year and by age twelve was employed at Orr's wallpaper factory for $1.25 a week. A few years and several jobs later he found employment at the stove foundry of Johnson, Cox & Co. where he worked in the molding room for two years.

Young John Morrissey grew tough through his manual labor and led Troy's "Down Town" gang as a seventeen-year-old in 1848. Morrissey referred to himself as the leader or "Chief Devil," and his main rivals were 24-year-old John O'Rourke and 26-year-old John Mackey, the leaders of the "Up Town" gang.[i]

O'Rourke was well known as a powerful man and a fearsome fighter who had "whipped everyone in the surrounding country."[ii]

In the fall of 1848, Morrissey happened to encounter an

John Morrissey

intoxicated and belligerent O'Rourke in Troy's common square. O'Rourke struck the first blow, allegedly without warning or provocation, and the two young toughs clinched. Before any telling blows could be landed O'Rourke's companions separated the two young toughs.

Several days later, however, Morrissey and O'Rourke met again in Lawrence's Saloon on River Street. O'Rourke charged Morrissey, and this time no one interfered. When the fight was finished, Morrissey had decisively defeated O'Rourke and earned local hero status. But the fight wasn't over. Eight of O'Rourke's chosen supporters challenged Morrissey, and the young man was forced to fight and defeat them successively. In the process, Morrissey established a national reputation as a fighting man.

One of his peers described Morrissey's fighting abilities: "John never seemed to know when he was licked, and, just as you got tired of thumping him, he kind o' got his second wind, and then you might as well tackle the devil as to try to make any headway against him."[iii]

Young and strapping, the six-foot-tall Morrissey proceeded to take on a variety of jobs including ironworker, whorehouse bouncer, and steamboat hand. While working on a steamboat, Morrissey met his future wife, the captain's daughter Susie Smith.

In 1849 Morrissey left Troy and traveled to New York City in the hopes of improving his lot in life and of making a name for himself with his fists.

He later recalled that time: "I was a river-boy, handling baggage and running for passengers, and very ambitious with very little opportunity. I had read of [Tom] Hyer and [Yankee] Sullivan, and the great pugilists in New York, and one day I took my bundle, came to the city, determined to get a fight out of them."[iv]

Upon arriving in New York, Morrissey went to the Empire Club on Park Row, the hangout for the notorious ruffian Isaiah Rynders, who was fervently anti-immigration and whom Morrissey described as a "famous political leader in them days."[v] Morrissey approached Rynders, who was surrounded by his equally roughneck associates, and said, "Mr. Rynders, I've come down here from Troy to fight. I've got no money, but I will fight for reputation. I will fight Mr. Hyer, or you, or anybody you can pick out."[vi]

His invitation brought an immediate response. The crowd of toughs jumped Morrissey and gave him a severe beating that in Morrisey's own words "made my head sore for three weeks."[vii] Having been laid up for several months, Morrissey vowed vengeance and struck back. "After that I laid for them individually ... Gentlemen, I will lick your crowd, and make you acknowledge me, if it takes me years," he said.[viii]

While he was successful in tracking down and beating the men from the Empire Club, he was unable to arrange a fight with either Tom Hyer, the acknowledged champion prizefighter of America, or Yankee Sullivan, another prominent prizefighter.

In the fall of 1850, as gold fever swept the country, Morrissey left New York for California with Daniel "Dad" Cunningham, a fellow gambler who was notorious for shooting and killing a man.

Pooling their funds, a total of $13, Morrissey and Cunningham successfully stowed away on the steamer *Panama* but were discovered when Morrissey saw a well-dressed man strike a young crew member and interceded. The boy sprawled at Morrissey's feet, and Morrissey reprimanded the gentleman, "You hadn't ought to strike a boy like that."[ix]

The gentleman blustered and threatened to have Morrissey put in irons. The man identified himself as the ship's captain and demanded to know who Morrissey was. Fortunately for Morrissey a commotion on the boat just at that moment allowed him to slip away from the confrontation, at least temporarily. Three days later, however, Morrissey was discovered when the purser, the captain, and his officers went around to collect the passengers' tickets.

Remembering the incident just a few days prior, the captain threatened to put the stowaways ashore at Acapulco — 1,500 miles from San Francisco. Before the captain could make good on his threat, fortune interceded when a group of thugs on the crowded ship organized a mutiny. Desperately seeking to re-establish control of the ship, the captain turned to the two stowaways and asked whether they would stand with him against the mutineers.

When Morrissey and Cunningham agreed, each was armed with a cutlass and a revolver. As the mutineers approached the captain and his officers, they saw the imposing Morrissey standing with the captain. It made the mutineers take pause, and one of the mutineers shouted at Morrissey, asking what he was doing supporting the captain. Morrissey replied, "Cold steel and hot lead for them as endeavor to pass this line."[x] Sensing his steely resolve, the mutineers quickly grew fainthearted and dispersed. For their efforts the captain put Morrissey and Cunningham up in a stateroom and gave them passage to San Francisco.

In San Francisco, Morrissey and Cunningham started a faro game and operated it successfully for several months. It was also in San Francisco that Morrissey had his first official bare-knuckle prizefight.

An English fighter by the name of George Thompson had recently won a match in San Francisco and afterward had issued a standing offer to anyone in California. When Thompson learned of Morrissey's arrival, a bare-knuckle fight was arranged for $1,000 a side. At that time professional prizefighting was illegal, so fights were usually held at locations beyond the law: islands, barges, and remote sites. The fight took place on Mare Island in San Francisco Bay in August 1852. After ten minutes of fighting, Thompson was disqualified.

With the victory, Morrissey returned east in November 1852 and sought to further his pugilistic career. On the day he landed in New York, he challenged Tom Hyer to fight for $10,000.

With his challenge, Morrissey finally captured the attention of Hyer, who had gone into semiretirement. But Hyer, along with his friend and fellow fighter Bill Poole, answered Morrissey's challenge with a surprise attack on the young fighter. Morrissey escaped Hyer's attempt to put him in his place and continued looking for prizefights. As Morrissey pondered his next match, he became enamored with a bordello madam and was forced to fight her former companion, Thomas McCann, for her attention. McCann was known as the champion prizefighter of New York City.

The two men fought in an old barroom at Leonard Street and Broadway. It was a furious fight, and at one point a coal furnace was knocked over in the brawl. As the smoking embers spilled out on the floor, McCann managed to pin Morrissey against the burning coals.

With the stench of burning flesh filling the room, McCann and the attending crowd expected Morrissey to surrender. But Morrissey refused to yield. He managed to throw McCann off and beat him senseless. From that day on Morrissey would be known as "Old Smoke."[xi]

With his San Francisco faro experience, Morrissey arranged to go into business with John Petrie, the owner of a Church Street gaming house, as an assistant manager. It was a profession in which he would prosper.

Soon afterward Morrissey opened a "sporting" house on Broadway known as the "Gem"[xii] near the old Broadway Theatre and also bought an interest in a Leonard Street casino, the Bella Union.

Morrissey had learned the tricks and techniques of card playing from his friend and fellow gambler "Dad" Cunningham and mastered the games of faro, roulette, monte, and dice. His poker play was said to be daring and shrewd, and Morrissey, who lived and drank as hard as he hit, was reported to have won vast amounts of money in games that lasted several days.

While he established himself as a successful gambler, Morrissey also pursued a match with Hyer. A tentative fight date was scheduled for November 1853 at The Abbey, near McComb's Dam. When Hyer appeared, he refused to fight, except with pistols. In fact, Hyer would never consent to fight Morrissey in the ring, and Morrissey said later, "Hyer I never could bring to the scratch. He had lost his moral force, and never would fight me."[xiii] While Hyer continued to dodge Morrissey, Hyer's good friend Bill Poole would turn out to be more than accommodating.

Morrissey's next fight was with Yankee Sullivan, whose only loss had been to Tom Hyer. In the eyes of the public, Hyer's continued refusal to fight caused him to relinquish his claim as America's champion prizefighter; therefore, the fight between Sullivan and Morrissey was generally acknowledged to be for the championship.

To avoid the law, the fight between Morrissey and Sullivan was scheduled for October 12, 1853, at the Boston Corners station of the Harlem Railroad, a hundred miles north of New York City. The small village, resting on the border between New York and Massachusetts, had no local law enforcement.

On fight day Morrissey appeared wearing stars and stripes for his colors. But the crowd's eyes were fixed on Yankee Sullivan's corner as his handlers placed a black kerchief on a stake, warning Morrissey and his supporters that Sullivan fought for victory or death.

Sullivan was considerably older and allegedly a heavy drinker and a thief. Sullivan also was known to have a vicious streak, but in the ring he was skillful and courageous. For much of the fight, Sullivan punished his younger and more inexperienced antagonist.

After thirty-six grueling rounds, however, Morrissey pushed the rapidly tiring Sullivan against the ropes. Sullivan's seconds jumped into the ring, a general brawl ensued, and referee Charley Allaire signaled that the round was over. When Sullivan failed to show for the next round — Sullivan was outside the ring fighting with one of Morrissey's seconds — Sullivan was counted out, and Morrissey became the new champion, a title he held until 1857.

After the fight Sullivan reportedly said of Morrissey, "You might as well hit a brick wall as hit that man on the head."[xiv]

Morrissey called it the hardest fight he had ever had, stating, "He was an artist, and he broke my nose, and cut me all to pieces; but I have always known that I could keep my legs and stand up until any of my opponents were worn out."[xv]

The Tammany Society sachems took notice of the proven fighting abilities of the young brawler from Troy who, like many other Irish immigrants, relied on the Tammany Society as a means to promote himself in life.

Tammany was the popular name for the Democratic political machine that played a major role in New York City politics from the 1790s to the 1960s. In its inception it was also a social club, but after 1798 the Tammany Society evolved as an important political organization that represented itself as the guardian of the common man and woman.

To bolster its support, the Tammany Society made a policy of recruiting newly arrived Irish Catholic immigrants, many of whom were fleeing the potato blight. These immigrants were given assistance in finding jobs and becoming naturalized. Of course, they were encouraged to vote for Tammany Society political candidates.

With the backing of newly arrived immigrants, the Tammany political organization became very successful in electing its candidates to office, beginning with the mayoral victory of Fernando Wood in 1854 through the election of Fiorello LaGuardia in 1934.

By the 1860s many of New York City's approximately 800,000 residents were Irish born and lacking specialized work skills. As a result, these newly arrived immigrants, most of them illiterate and poor, became the focus of a simmering resentment among the native working force because the Irish were often perceived as lazy and drunken brutes who were little more than a second column for the Pope and who were taking their jobs away.

The anti-Irish sentiment manifested itself politically in the form of the Native American Party, which had evolved from the American Republic Party, formed in New York state in 1843.

The Native American Party was commonly known as the Know-Nothing Party because its members would often reply to questions, especially from law enforcement officers, with a blank look and an equally blank reply, "I know nothing." The Know Nothings advocated limiting immigration and routinely blamed the Irish immigrants for society's ills.

In New York City, the Tammany Hall politicians and those opposed to Tammany enlisted and sometimes paid street gangs to serve as political muscle. The gangs regularly threatened voters, stuffed or destroyed ballot boxes, and physically occupied polling places to ensure a certain political outcome. One prominent large gang, the Bowery B'hoys, was affiliated with the Know-Nothing Party and was considered a "nativist" gang for its anti-Irish stance. Another major gang, the Dead Rabbits, from the heavily Irish Five Points area, was affiliated with Tammany Hall.

One of Tammany's leaders, John Kennedy, called on Morrissey, and his talent for using his fists, to protect the ballot boxes in Tammany districts for the Tammany and Catholic mayoral candidate in 1854, Fernando Wood.

Morrissey gathered his gang friends to protect the voting booths in Kennedy's district from the Know-Nothing gangs who were sure to attempt to interfere. The Know-Nothing gangs were led by Tom Hyer's good friend William (Bill) Poole, aka "Butcher Bill," unquestionably the most lethal street fighter in New York City.

Bill Poole, the son of a butcher who had his own shop, was more than six feet tall, weighed about two hundred pounds, and was virulently anti-Catholic and anti-immigrant. Not unsurprisingly, he was also an expert in the use of butcher knives. It was said that he could throw a butcher knife through a pine plank at twenty feet.

Morrissey and a group of Dead Rabbits were assigned to protect a polling place from the Know Nothings. They had stationed themselves in the polling place early on election day and waited. Around noon a large lumber wagon rolled to a stop outside the polling place and Poole and his men jumped off. They entered the polling place expecting little or no resistance and instead found Morrissey and the armed Dead Rabbit gang members waiting. Poole took one look and promptly walked out, with his men following.

Thwarting Butcher Bill and his gang made Morrissey an instant folk hero for New York's Irish community as the man who had stood up to the reign of terror imposed by Poole's gang and other nativist gangs. The Tammany bosses were so pleased with Morrissey that he was welcomed into the Tammany fold and given his own gambling franchise free from government interference.

Within a few years Morrissey owned several Manhattan gambling houses, the most lavish at 5 West 24th Street, where he reportedly could earn as much as $2,000 a week. His fortune grew to be worth a half-million dollars, and he became America's best-known gambler.

Years later Morrissey was asked how he overcame his hardscrabble background to become a successful businessman and politician. Morrissey said he always had great confidence in himself. "That, I had a great deal of. I came to New York a stout lad, determined to fight, and to fight the biggest man that could be found. My father lived in Troy. I was the only boy in a family of eight, and had to support the girls, and I looked around me, very poor and very illiterate, and asked what I could do best of anything to get on. There was nothing I could think of but to fight ..."[xvi]

However, before Morrissey could attain the respect and respectability that he clearly desired, he had one more obstacle: his running feud with Bill Poole. The two men met again in a drinking place on Broadway, exchanged heated words, and agreed to settle the matter in a "rough and tumble"[xvii] fight.

On a sunny July morning in 1854 on the Amos Street dock, Morrissey arrived alone, but Poole was surrounded by several of his gang members. Morrissey threw the first punch, which missed badly, and the two men grappled. Soon the quicker Poole had Morrissey on the ground and pummeled him relentlessly. After several minutes of a bloody beating, Morrissey yielded, for the first and last time in his life.

The feud continued to simmer and in February 1855, Lew Baker, a friend of Morrissey, shot and mortally wounded Bill Poole in Stanwix Hall, a saloon on Broadway. Poole held on for almost two weeks, then died of his wounds.

With the elimination of a deadly foe and a successful gambling career and championship title in hand, Morrissey began to restrain in his alcohol use and pursued the attention of the attractive and well-educated Susie Smith — the steamboat captain's daughter he had met several years before. Morrissey married her, with the intention of leaving his fighting days behind.

But Morrissey's brawling past continued to haunt him. Another fighter, John Heenan, had built an impressive fighting reputation in California and challenged Morrissey. Heenan's supporters and the public applied pressure to force the fight, going so far as to harass Morrissey's family and make public declarations in the local newspapers. Morrissey's new wife abhorred boxing but allowed her husband to fight, with the stipulation that this prizefight would be his last. The fight was scheduled at Long Point, Canada, on the other side of Lake Erie from Long Island Point, outside of the New York City sheriff's jurisdiction. The New York press and the sporting press covered the upcoming fight extensively, and it was eagerly anticipated.

The fight was just into the third round when both men fell. In Round 8, Morrissey battered Heenan, who fell again. In Round 11, Morrissey hit Heenan so hard that the staggering Heenan swung wildly, collapsed, and struggled to reach his corner, from which he did not emerge. For his efforts Morrissey retained the title and won $2,500 and a side bet of as much as $5,000.

Morrissey then kept his word and promptly retired as the undefeated champ. But his violent past again loomed large when the vanquished Heenan insisted on a rematch. Heenan refused to let the matter drop, and Morrissey's refusal to offer a rematch rankled Heenan and his supporters. The sporting public considered Morrissey's refusal controversial, and he was subjected to public censure. Morrissey was even threatened by sneering crowds on the street, and because he made for such good copy, the newspapers repeatedly attempted to stir the champion out of retirement.

Later that year he responded to the threats, pressure, and criticism from the sporting media with a letter to the *New York Tribune*:

> My duties to my family and myself require me to devote my time and efforts to purposes more laudable and advantageous. I hope to be permitted to do so without interference from my late antagonist and his friends. I am aware of his published challenge and threat. It seems to be the determination to force me into another match or assail me openly with violence. I now repeat that I shall never enter the prize ring again, and those who know me will not misapprehend the motives for this resolution. It arises from no fear of any man but from a desire more fittingly to discharge my duties to my family and society. Nor shall I be driven from this purpose by any threats of unlawful violence. I shall trust to the laws and the just influence of public sentiment to preserve me in the common privileges of an American citizen.[xviii]

With this statement Morrissey made very clear his seriousness about making a break from his violent and shadowy past. The direction he was about to take became clear in 1861 when Morrissey and Susie first appeared at Saratoga Springs in upstate New York for a two-week visit. From there he again felt compelled to respond to the unrelenting pressure exerted by Heenan's supporters and the sporting press. Morrissey said, "I

Morrissey's vision paid off: Saratoga Race Course, circa 1867.

am not training for any fight, but am here for my health, and have business of more importance on hand than preparing for such a contest."[xix]

The "business" Morrissey had on his mind soon became evident. Morrissey had a vision for the construction in Saratoga of a gambling casino, whose splendor one day would rival the casinos of Monte Carlo, and a world-class racetrack. When Morrissey decided he was ready to begin organizing a race meet, he shrewdly parlayed on a local custom.

It could not have been a coincidence that Morrissey selected Saratoga as the site for his vision. Saratoga had a long and sometimes noteworthy trotting-horse tradition. Some of the most celebrated trotters in the land, such as the Old Grey Mare and Flora Temple, raced there.

But the passion for trotting seemed to be waning — it had been four years since Flora Temple had beaten Princess at the Saratoga

A remnant of the original track survives today as Horse Haven.

Trotting Course. Even with the past interest in high-profile trotting races, building a new racetrack was a risky venture. While Saratoga profited from the famous mineral springs, and as a destination for wealthy socialites, little precedent for organized horse racing existed in the community.

Yet Morrissey shrewdly sensed an opportunity and gambled on his dream. In May 1863, as the bloody and brutal war between the North and South raged on and a weary public looked for relief from wartime news, Morrissey placed advertisements in newspapers for a series of Thoroughbred races to be held that coming August at a course that had been built in 1847, the Saratoga Trotting Course.[xx] A remnant of the original track survives today as part of the Saratoga Race Course grounds and is known as Horse Haven.

For that first meeting in 1863, Morrissey would lease the land and put up $2,700 for prize money.[xxi] (Several weeks after the closing of the races the land was purchased for $7,108.75.)[xxii]

With the assistance of some well-heeled and influential

friends, such as Cornelius Vanderbilt, William R. Travers, and Leonard Jerome, Morrissey went about organizing the first race meeting at Saratoga in what was to become a fixture of the racing season, drawing the finest horses.

CHAPTER 2

Movers and Shakers

John Morrissey's notoriety as a public brawler, gang member, and professional gambler probably would have precluded any chance of his opening a business serving respectable clientele in Saratoga in the 1860s.

However, Morrissey's celebrity status did help him considerably improve his standing socially and professionally. In 1860 at a ball to honor the newly elected Abraham Lincoln, Mr. and Mrs. John Morrissey were among those presented to the president at New York City's Astor Hotel.

Morrissey also began to rub elbows with a group of wealthy businessmen who shared his interest in horse racing and Saratoga. To make himself more agreeable to the Turf set, and to further his vision for a world-class racetrack in Saratoga, Morrissey began crafting a new public image by enlisting patronage from a group of affluent and powerful men that included Cornelius Vanderbilt, William R. Travers, John R. Hunter, Leonard Jerome, and Jay Gould.[i] Morrissey, the former prizefighting champion, even purchased one of prominent Kentucky breeder John H. Clay's racehorses for $3,000 to run in the first event.[ii]

In addition to their wealth, these men were widely respected and admired for their shrewd ability to seize opportunities

Commodore Vanderbilt

created by a rapidly expanding American economy, and, as Morrissey did, Vanderbilt and Jerome embodied real-life rags-to-riches stories.

Cornelius (frequently known as "Commodore") Vanderbilt was blessed with size and strength, a photographic memory, a fiercely competitive nature, and an overwhelming drive for success and financial gain. In 1810, at the age of sixteen, Vanderbilt borrowed $100 from his father and bought a small two-masted, flat-bottomed boat that he operated as a ferry from Staten Island to Manhattan. Vanderbilt went on to amass a fortune building and operating a fleet of steamships.

Vanderbilt was unrelenting in his business pursuits and could be unforgiving if he felt crossed. In 1853 he was the only bondholder of the Accessory Transit Company and was perceived as its future director. When he decided to take some time off for relaxation with a voyage on his yacht, he left the company in the hands of two associates, Charles Morgan and Cornelius K. Garrison.

Soon after Vanderbilt's yacht, the *North Star*, sailed to Europe, news reached Vanderbilt that the two men had conspired to usurp control of the company and manipulated the stock on the stock exchange. After learning of the attempt to wrest control from him, Vanderbilt promptly responded with a letter to Morgan and Garrison, "You have undertaken to cheat me. I won't sue you, for the law is too slow. I'll ruin you."[iii] Vanderbilt made good on his threat. The two men, compelled to settle with him, later were forced out of the company.

In 1844, at age forty-nine, the six-foot-one Vanderbilt organized a political march in New York City in support of presidential candidate Henry Clay.

Yankee Sullivan, an ardent Tammany man and a champion fighter, threatened to break up Vanderbilt's parade. Sullivan eagerly boasted he could "thrash" any of the Clay supporters on sight.[v]

On the day of the parade, Sullivan and a gang of thugs emerged from a saloon and headed straight for Vanderbilt, who was leading the parade on horseback. Sullivan grabbed the reins to force Vanderbilt to dismount. To Sullivan's surprise and dismay, Vanderbilt quickly jumped from his horse and proceeded to pummel the prizefighter into a "nearly senseless condition"[vi] as his fellow horsemen held off Sullivan's gang.

While physically courageous, Vanderbilt also possessed the courage to forge ahead with new ideas. When technological innovation created a superior and more cost-effective mode of transportation in the steam rail engine, the sixty-plus-year-old Vanderbilt began to create a fortune in the railroad industry.

In 1862 Vanderbilt began buying shares of the New York and Harlem Railroad at $8 per share. In his attempt to establish a railroad empire, Vanderbilt gathered a group of wealthy investors to purchase the railroad.

Vanderbilt, gruff and earthy, also was the link between these wealthy industrialists and Morrissey. The exact date when the two met is uncertain, but it is likely they became friendly when Morrissey began to dabble in the stock market in 1861.[iv]

Morrissey's friendship with Vanderbilt grew into a business relationship when Morrissey also was brought into the railroad project. The *New York Times* described Morrissey as "known the country over"[vii] as he became Vanderbilt's "political agent"[viii] to help build the Harlem Railroad.

Leonard Jerome

In summers the empire-building Vanderbilt took time from his business interests and relaxed at Saratoga. He usually spent the entire summer there playing whist and euchre on the piazzas, mulling over the fate of the railroad empire he was building, and sending his agents to place bets on the stock market.

Saratoga also provided an outlet for Vanderbilt's interest in championship-caliber trotters. Vanderbilt was devoted to his prized trotters and built a stable for them on Fourth Street in New York City near his Washington Place residence. Late in the afternoon Bloomingdale Road regularly was the scene of impromptu races between fast trotters owned by some of the city's wealthiest men, including Vanderbilt and Robert Bonner.

Bonner regularly raced his best team of Flatbush Maid and Lady Palmer against Vanderbilt's favorite team of Plow Boy and Post Boy, with Bonner's team usually prevailing.

Vanderbilt didn't confine his trotters to informal races with friends on the streets of New York. Frequently his trotters were involved in important races with some of the more noted harness horses of the time.

Vanderbilt was so proud of his trotters that he regularly brought them along when he vacationed in Saratoga, which had become a hotbed for trotting. In 1847 local businessmen had built the first trotting track in Saratoga, the Saratoga Trotting Course, on Union Avenue, and it proved so popular that several other tracks subsequently opened and closed.

Common interests and personality traits bonded the racing entrepreneur Morrissey and Vanderbilt. Both men were by nature courageous and earthy; they loved to gamble and were very fond of women. They also had an interest in Saratoga's prominence as a resort. Eventually, Vanderbilt started feeding Morrissey stock market tips, and Morrissey often spent his days away from the track and casino, at the Congress Hall telegraph office watching his investments.

The Vanderbilt connection was essential to Morrissey's plans to bring horse racing to Saratoga. It was extremely unlikely that influential businessmen such as William Travers, Jay Gould, John Hunter, and Leonard Jerome would associate with a man who had John Morrissey's background unless he had had the backing of a stock market titan such as Cornelius Vanderbilt.

Through Vanderbilt, Morrissey had met Harlem Railroad partner Leonard Jerome.[ix] Jerome, a Saratoga regular, was a wealthy businessman and lawyer with a passion for horses

The great racehorse Kentucky

William Travers

and racing. Like Vanderbilt, Jerome was a survivor, and often a winner, in the tumultuous early days of the stock market.

In the 1850s Jerome entered into business on New York's Wall Street with his brother Addison and another lawyer, William Travers. The firm was successful in generating wealth for Travers and the Jerome brothers. The pressures of the market, however, led to turbulent machinations in which fortunes were sometimes won and lost in a matter of hours. Jerome described these Wall Street battles as "a jungle where men tear and claw."[x]

Perhaps as an escape from the pressures of the market, Jerome also doted on his trotters. Jerome's love of horses and horse racing gave rise to the belief that all of his spare time was devoted to his pair of horses. An article in the *New York Tribune* reported:

"His passion for the theatre and opera was only surpassed by his love of horses. He built his stable before he built his house. It was of brick, faced with marble, three stories high, with a mansard roof. He filled it with horses and carriages of the finest makes. Except for the Emperor's Mews in Paris, it is doubtful if any stable in the world at that time surpassed Jerome's. Black walnut, plate glass, carpeted floors and other costly decorations ornamented the place. Above the stable he built a private theatre, handsomely adorned."[xi]

It was directly in front of the stable that Jerome built his spacious home. When the Jeromes moved into their new house, he brought carriage horses, champion hacks, and two fast trotters.

With his wealth, Jerome was a player, and in 1865 he would become a partner in a group to buy the superior runner Kentucky, a son of the great sire Lexington, from Travers and Hunter.

When they weren't gambling together or working on creating a railroad empire, Vanderbilt, Jerome, and Morrissey were seen socializing together. On good days Vanderbilt often raced his trotters on Harlem Lane from Central Park to 162nd Street and Jerome Avenue. His racing partners included Jerome and Morrissey, and the three became fast friends.

Anita Leslie, Jerome's great-granddaughter, commented on Morrissey's relationship with the business tycoons: "Since Jerome had entered as Vanderbilt's partner in the Harlem railroad, the three men were often seen together. Well-bred folks disapproved but could not resist watching as the suave intruder with the broken nose matched his horses in Harlem Lane against those of Vanderbilt, Jerome, and Belmont."[xii]

Another of the prominent individuals whom Morrissey named as a backer was Jerome's business partner, William Travers, who also was involved in horse racing. He owned Annieswood Stable in Westchester County, New York, in partnership with Westchester sportsman John R. Hunter and George Osgood, a Vanderbilt in-law, and the place became known for producing quality racehorses. In 1869 Hunter would breed the bay colt, Alarm, who would become a great American sprinter.

As experts of the Turf, Vanderbilt, Jerome, and Travers became the key players in Morrissey's plan to establish Thoroughbred racing at Saratoga. Morrissey actually put up most of the original money (in all likelihood money he had accrued from his days in New York City gambling houses or as a professional prize fighter), including money for the purses, but might have decided that as much as New York society did not consider him sufficiently respectable for Saratoga, he would remain behind the scenes. Because Travers, Hunter, and Jerome were men of prestige, Morrissey decided to keep his name from any of the official documents attached to the track and let these men head the project. Without Morrissey's overt association, the idea of a racetrack had little trouble being accepted by the Saratoga citizenry.

Travers, Hunter, and Jerome later became the core of the Saratoga Racing Association (with Travers as president) that laid out plans for the first Thoroughbred racetrack at Saratoga. But first, a four-day trial meet, comprising eight races, was scheduled for August 1863 at the old Saratoga Trotting Course, the remnants of which today are known as Horse Haven.

To ensure a successful racing program, Morrissey shrewdly hired an acknowledged authority on racetracks, Charles Wheatly. At the time, Wheatly was the secretary and manager of the Kentucky Association track in Lexington. With Wheatly in charge, the chances of Morrissey's vision to bring racing to Saratoga were augmented significantly.

CHAPTER 3

The First Meeting

In mid-July 1863, just a few weeks before the inaugural Thoroughbred race meeting at Saratoga, the list of nominated horses ran in *Wilkes' Spirit of the Times,* a paper devoted to sporting issues.[i] The list included some of the more established names in racing at that time, such as three-year-old filly Lizzie W., five-year-old John Morgan, four-year-old Thunder, and three-year-old Captain Moore.

However, a drugging scandal involving the highly regarded John Morgan put his attendance at Saratoga on precarious footing.

On June 10 at the Philadelphia meet, John Morgan, a son of Sovereign, owned by Frank G. Murphy of Kentucky, finished second to the outstanding mare Idlewild in a two-mile heat race. (The previous May, John Morgan had defeated Idlewild at the Paterson, New Jersey, track.) Three days later, on the meet's final day, John Morgan again appeared, this time in a four-mile race against another leading contender of the day, the four-year-old colt Jerome Edgar.

The race, much anticipated because it featured two strong runners with proven endurance, was notable only for the lackluster and, perhaps, suspicious performance of John

Saratoga's grandstand circa 1885, twenty-two years after the first meet

Morgan. He had run well on the first day, but on this day he ran very poorly for the first three and a half miles before stopping abruptly. It was only with great difficulty that the sluggish and unresponsive John Morgan could be guided off the course.

Following the meeting, John Morgan remained ill despite treatment from a prominent veterinarian, and his owner debated whether to withdraw the horse from the upcoming Saratoga meeting. Rumors that John Morgan had been drugged at the

Philadelphia meeting to prevent him from winning immediately spread through the racing community; however, nothing was ever substantiated.

Preparations for the inaugural meeting at Saratoga were further disrupted with the news that Idlewild's owner, Captain T.G. Moore, had requested the one-eyed mare be allowed to have a match race there. On June 25, Idlewild, with jockey Tommy Patton aboard, had smashed the American record for three miles at Centreville, Long Island, besting the legendary Fashion's record by six seconds. Idlewild had run the distance in 5:27 1/4, beating John Edgar and another prominent runner of the day, Dangerous.

In 1863 Idlewild and Frances Morris' chestnut horse Reporter, two of the leading horses in America, were engaged in a heated duel that had captured the public's fancy. The races between Idlewild and Reporter were prominently covered in the press and drew large crowds. Idlewild had just established a new three-mile record; Reporter, sired by Lexington out of a dam by American Eclipse, was also well thought of and described as "no handsomer horse is stripped upon the courses."[ii]

At the Paterson spring meeting Reporter defeated Idlewild and John Morgan in the two-mile heats. Idlewild next appeared against Reporter and John Morgan at Philadelphia on June 11, where she avenged her defeat to Reporter in what was described as a "dreadful lathering."[iii]

Despite Moore's request for a match race between Idlewild and Reporter, Morrissey had established a policy not to allow such matches. The decision was not well received and *Wilkes' Spirit of the Times* reported: "We could have wished, for the sake of the ladies, that Idlewild had not been excluded from all the races at Saratoga. The achievements of this famous one-eyed mare have been so great — her eminence as the champion racer of America is so lofty, that the fashionable belles of the Springs would much delight to see her run. As the case stands, she will not be there, and there is no remedy, unless somebody has got a horse that they would be willing to match against her, any distance from one mile to four, for any reasonable sum. Who speaks?"[iv]

Without Idlewild, the current American three-mile record holder, the competition in the Congress Spring three-mile heat race, scheduled for August 5, would suffer. Apparently the decision not to allow a match race caused some negative feedback from Idlewild's owner; a subsequent list of races and nominated horses for the first Saratoga meet included a special note that stated "in all the above races 'Idlewild' excluded."[v]

◆◆◆◆

Admission for Saratoga's opening day, August 3, 1863, was $1. Turf historian Edward Hotaling estimated the crowd at 3,000. Lines of private carriages extended at least a mile from the racetrack as people waited to enter the grounds, and the grandstand filled with spectators eager to see the country's top horses and jockeys. Hotaling speculated that the large crowd allowed Morrissey to recover the $2,700 he had provided for purse money.[vi] The racetrack, according to *Wilkes' Spirit of the Times*, was a mile out of town in a picturesque setting. The stables overlooked a rich, cultivated valley, many miles in width, to purple hills curtained with light summer haze far beyond. But the course itself was not well calculated for racing purposes. It was too narrow, and the turns too sharp to be good for the horses. A sandy knoll covered with a growth of small scrub pines obstructed spectator views, as did maples and pines lining the course. Stables and other buildings masked the far turn.[vii]

The old harness track's circumference measured short of one mile, but Morrissey had proclaimed that for the new meeting once around would be considered a mile. In fact, the track was

297 yards short of a mile[viii], designed with long straight sections and tight turns and a width of only sixty-six feet.[ix] The track area was not fenced in, and the surface was not graded.[x] The grandstand was small and had no places for the ladies in attendance to sit; most just watched from their carriages. Prior to the meet, parties were held to herald the event. The steamer *Francis Skiddy*, which had been reserved for a trip on the Hudson to bring eager fans to Saratoga, was the scene of continuing celebration. *Wilkes' Spirit of the Times* described the merriment: "There was choice anecdote, joyous joke and much hilarity. Hour after hour some fell away and sought their state-rooms, until when the morn stood tip-toe on the mountain-tops, only a few choice spirits remained on the deck."[xi]

In anticipation of the races, Dr. Robert Underwood, a veterinarian from Kentucky and sometime breeder and seller, was already selling shares in the pools for the races for a 3 percent commission.[xii] His customers bid on the right to bet in the pool on certain horses in the various races, and the winning bids for all the horses made up the total amount of money that could be won. For gamblers it was very risky because the odds were not available until all the bets had been made.[xiii]

It was also very expensive because the winning bids for the horses perceived as favorites were usually several hundred dollars. Still, to commemorate the first races at Saratoga, Underwood offered to reduce somewhat the amount of money bid on the horses. *Wilkes' Spirit of the Times* reported, "Doctor Underwood [is] knocking down pools for a matter of ten dollars by which the lucky purchaser is finally entitled to the receipt of some seven or eight hundred."[xiv]

The first day of racing began with a one-mile heat sweepstakes for three-year-olds, a $1,000 winner-take-all contest, with winners at Paterson or Philadelphia to carry five pounds extra. The entry fee was $200 with $300 added; eight horses had been nominated to run, but six paid the forfeit of $50.

The competition had been considered so challenging that most of the owners had pulled their horses. *Wilkes' Spirit of the Times* reported, "Only two came to the post, viz: Captain Moore and Lizzie W. The reputation of both is exceedingly great. The colt has all along been held the best of the year, and is, beyond doubt, a strong, game and very fleet horse. The filly is so good that many thought, good as the colt was, she could clip him."[xv]

James S. Watson owned Captain Moore and named the colt for Captain T.G. Moore, owner of Idlewild. Captain Moore, a son of Balrownie out of the Glencoe mare Jenny Rose, was ridden by Billy Burgoyne, who recently had fractured his leg at Centreville but still managed to ride on Saratoga's opening day.

Dr. J.W. Weldon of Missouri owned Lizzie W. He had acquired her "dirt cheap"[xvi] and had gotten a good return on his investment with her three earlier wins that year. Lizzie W., a daughter of Scythian out of a Glencoe mare, was under the "one-eyed black boy" Sewell.[xvii]

At 11:30 a.m. the signal for the first heat was given. Captain Moore grabbed the lead on the rail and took the advantage into the turn. Then, for whatever reason, Captain Moore "took to the sulks,"[xviii] and Lizzie W. moved past him. She kept a lead of two lengths going into the backstretch.

On the backstretch Burgoyne managed to collect Captain Moore and push him back into the race. At the far turn the re-energized Captain Moore drew even. Down the stretch Lizzie W. and Captain Moore fought each other neck and neck, and at the finish line it was Billy Burgoyne and Captain Moore in 1:29 1/2, a time that corresponded to 1:47 1/2 for a full mile (the race times had to be extrapolated because the track length fell short of a mile).

After a twenty-minute rest period, the horses and jockeys

lined up for the second heat. With his victory in the first heat, Captain Moore was a decided favorite in the betting. Six-to-one odds were offered in his favor, but there were no takers from Lizzie W.'s supporters.

◆◆◆◆

After the first heat, Sewell had been instructed to allow Captain Moore to lead to the stretch and at that point make his move with the filly. As expected, Captain Moore set the pace and led by a length in the stretch, when Sewell had Lizzie W. challenge him. As Lizzie W. made her move, Captain Moore appeared to falter, and Lizzie W. managed to pull even. At the finish the filly pulled ahead by a neck, in 1:32, which corresponded to a full mile in 1:50 1/4.

Despite losing the second heat, Captain Moore was still favored in the betting to take the third heat and was backed at 4-5. With success in the second heat, Sewell was again instructed to allow Captain Moore to set the pace and take the lead going into the stretch. Captain Moore jumped ahead with a "splitting pace"[xix] just as Lizzie W.'s supporters had hoped. Sewell again had Lizzie W. wait until the stretch before she made her move, and she pulled ahead to take the lead. As Lizzie W. passed him, Captain Moore again resorted to sulking and refused to challenge down the stretch. The filly won the heat — and the race — in 1:30 1/2, which corresponded to a 1:48 1/2 full mile.

The second race, a two-mile dash for all ages, featured the undefeated Thunder, a Kentucky-bred son of Lexington, owned by Dennis Reedy and Major W. Hogan of Montreal, Canada. It was expected that Thunder's main competition would come from Jerome Edgar, whom Thunder had beaten earlier that season. Morrissey had recently acquired Jerome Edgar, a son of Star Davis, from owner John Clay, son of the famous Kentucky senator Henry Clay, for $3,000 and renamed the colt John B. Davidson. The renaming was perhaps Morrissey's attempt to conceal the colt's ability, but that didn't fool Saratoga's knowledgeable patrons, who made John B. Davidson the favorite. Given Thunder's unblemished record, perhaps the favoritism had more to do with the race's jockeys. John B. Davidson was ridden by the acclaimed rider Gilbert Watson Patrick, more commonly known as Gilpatrick. In his mid-forties and one of the most accomplished jockeys of his time, Gilpatrick had ridden two of the best horses of the nineteenth century, Boston and Lexington, and had been honored to accompany owner Richard Ten Broeck to England to ride Prioress, who had established herself in racing history as the first American-bred and -owned horse to win a race in England.

On this day, however, the talented Gilpatrick was matched against a young and inexperienced Canadian jockey named Jesse, who rode Thunder. Thunder took the lead with a "splitting pace,"[xx] gaining four lengths over John B. Davidson into the stretch, with the fillies Sympathy and Echo farther back. Going into the final turn, Thunder still had a sizeable lead, and odds of 10-1 were offered in his favor.

The young Canadian jockey's inexperience came back to haunt Thunder's camp in the homestretch, as the *Wilkes' Spirit of the Times* report noted. "If his rider had taken a strong pull on him, even then he could not have lost it."[xxi] But Thunder's exhausting pace wore him out, and the colt labored in the stretch run. Both John B. Davidson and Sympathy caught him, and all three horses struggled down the stretch as the jockeys whipped and spurred furiously. At the finish it was the filly by a neck, John B. Davidson second by a neck over Thunder, and Echo several lengths back. The winning time was 3:02, which corresponded to 3:38 1/2 for a full two miles.

After the race, *Wilkes' Spirit of the Times* observed that the trackside consensus was John B. Davidson had not been in prime condition and Thunder had been badly ridden. But the young Canadian jockey may not have been totally to blame. Before the race he had been told to set the pace and to lead from start to finish. Sympathy, an older full sister to Lizzie W., had won because she ran gamely and had the most stamina, giving her owner, J.W. Weldon, a victory in both races on the first day.

Henry Price McGrath

The second day's races drew an even larger crowd, and carriages and eager spectators packed the area near the homestretch. The day's highlights included a victory by favored John Morgan in a three-heat mile contest, in which he took all three heats.

In the day's second race, Seven Oaks, a four-year-old filly by Vandal, took a two-and-a-half-mile handicap stakes. Morrissey had asked his old friend and gambling partner, Henry Price McGrath, to assign weights for the race. McGrath, who would found McGrathiana Stud near Lexington, Kentucky, and who would breed the first Kentucky Derby winner, Aristides, was so adept at assigning weights that he had created much indecision in the betting. Seven Oaks, with Sewell up, had been assigned eighty-five pounds to top-weight Ben West's 104. A well-known sprinter, Ben West was suffering from a cracked hoof that had disrupted his workouts. In the handicap stakes, the weight appeared to be too much for him, and he finished third.

The meet's third day featured a stakes for three-year-olds at two miles and was won by James Watson's Aldebaran, a chestnut son of Commodore out of the Glencoe mare Nannie Lewis. In the other race of the day, Captain Moore and the five-year-old mare Mammoma met in a best three of five heats at one mile. In the first heat Captain Moore took an early lead and had plenty left to hold off Mammoma when she challenged in the stretch.

All morning the skies had grown darker, and rain threatened at any moment. Before the horses could line up for the second heat, a furious rainstorm swept through the area, leaving the track muddy with a few standing pools of water. Once the storm had passed, Captain Moore and Mammoma were sent out for the second heat. Again Captain Moore prevailed, even though Mammoma had gotten closer to him in the stretch.

However, most observers believed the rainstorm had changed the dynamics of the race. Mammoma was known not to race well on an off track. Captain Moore, on the other hand, had the look of a good mudder, and his jockey, Billy Burgoyne, dismissed all doubts about his horse as the rain swept through, saying, "I had his mother and she was a rattling good mud-nag."[xxii]

Before the horses lined up for the third heat, all the money was on Captain Moore. The colt jumped out in front, was never headed, and won easily in 1:32, or 1:50 1/4 for a full mile.

The last day of the inaugural meet, August 6, 1863, fell on the same day President Lincoln marked as a day of thanksgiving for the recent Union victory at Gettysburg. It also marked the first major scandal at the Saratoga track, one involving the recently defeated Thunder.

Another large crowd had appeared and eagerly awaited the $500 two-mile heats for all ages in which John B. Davidson, Thunder, John Morgan, and Sympathy were scheduled to compete.

It had been hoped that John B. Davidson would have another opportunity to face off against Sympathy and Thunder after the thrilling finish on the first day. But by this time Morrissey's colt was deemed unable to run and was withdrawn.

Much money was riding on this race, and most of the early money had been placed on John Morgan, though Thunder still had his share of supporters and Sympathy pulled in a little action as well. In the grand ballroom of the United States Hotel on the eve of the race, Dr. Underwood had held court with one of his betting pools, in which Sympathy's support grew.

But by the next morning, all the "smart" money seemed to be heading for Thunder. Under Tommy Patton, who usually rode Idlewild, Thunder was paired with the sprinter Ben West, for the morning exercise. No one really believed that Thunder could keep up with Ben West over a shorter distance, even in warm-ups, much less beat him. But in the workout Patton actually had to pull up the colt from Canada when it became apparent that he had more than enough speed to stay with Ben West. Afterward, Patton said Thunder ran "like blazes"[xxiii] and was sure to win that day.

Thunder's morning workout started a mad dash among gamblers to place money on him. The mad dash came to an abrupt halt, however, after the colt was returned to his stall and his groom found chunks of an apple laced with an unidentified substance on the colt's muzzle. Because the apple was not intact, it was almost certain that Thunder had consumed at least some of the substance.

An intrepid individual sampled the apple chunks and found the taste hot and bitter, indicating without a doubt the presence of a foreign substance. Thunder's connections then decided to send the apple chunks immediately to the nearest chemist, in Troy or Albany. But as it was almost race time, there would be no time to wait for the results. Thunder's connections decided that despite his exceptional morning performance, the colt might have swallowed some of the unknown substance and could be in great jeopardy if he ran.

Co-owner and trainer Dennis Reedy asked to be allowed to

Saratoga Race Course, circa 1890s

withdraw his horse. The judges examined the colt and found his eyes bright and his motion easy. But the judges agreed that the risk was too great and indicated that Thunder could be withdrawn from the race.

Thunder's backers, who just moments before were so eager to gamble their money on the colt from Canada, were bitterly disappointed. Even his jockey, Tommy Patton, who was suited and eager to ride, ruefully remarked as Thunder was led away, "I could beat that pair far enough with him, for I don't believe he got enough of the apple to stop him."[xxiv]

The crowd was still buzzing about the mysterious withdrawal of the promising colt when the two remaining horses were led to the starting line. Sympathy appeared with Gilpatrick aboard and John Morgan with Hafferty up. In the first heat John

Morgan took the lead and was two lengths ahead after the first mile. In the second mile on the backstretch Gilpatrick allowed the filly to move up to Morgan's haunches, where he kept her. As they approached the stretch, Gilpatrick let Sympathy run again, and she easily passed John Morgan in no more than three or four strides to win by a length in time of 3:08 1/2, or 3:46 for two full miles.

After Sympathy's brilliant performance in the first heat, no one would offer money against her in the second heat. At the start John Morgan again jumped out to lead through the first mile by as much as two lengths. Sympathy again waited until the second mile on the backstretch before making her move and pulled up to his haunches. After a hard-fought struggle down the homestretch, she pulled ahead at the finish to win the heat, and the race, in time of 3:13 1/2, or 3:52 for a full two miles.

Afterward, fans, observers, and many gamblers wondered whether Thunder would have won if not for the apple and foreign substance.

Apparently, the night before, Thunder had been put in his stall at the course, with two "boys"[xxiv] assigned to watch him. They slept in an adjacent stall, but the stall on the other side was empty, with a space over the door by which someone might enter and then climb over the partition between stalls.

When trainer Reedy was asked about the incident, he replied that when he went to check on his horse that evening, he had seen three men lurking near the stables. As he approached, the strangers immediately ran into the bushes and out of sight. When the perturbed Reedy was asked if he thought that the colt had been given more than one apple, he exclaimed, "No! It is not at all likely that the scoundrels used more than one. This thing was done in a hurry."[xvi]

◆◆◆◆

Despite the incident with Thunder, the four days of racing

had proven very successful. The meet received national press and drew spectators from across the country. Approximately 15,000 paid their $1 admission to see the races.[xxvii]

Given the trial meet's success, Morrissey, Jerome, and the others moved ahead with their plans to develop Thoroughbred racing there. On August 26, 1863, the Saratoga Racing Association was formed. To head the group, William Travers was brought in as president. Leonard Jerome was selected as the vice president, and John F. Purdy, a wine dealer and gentleman jockey, was named the second vice president.

An executive committee comprised John Hunter, a Westchester sportsman and stable owner; Erastus Corning, the president of the New York Central Railroad; George A. Osgood, Cornelius Vanderbilt's son-in-law and a railroad executive; James Marvin, the owner of the United States Hotel; and John Davidson, a Hudson riverboat operator and personal friend of Morrissey. Morrissey and Wheatly were selected to manage the daily operations, with Wheatly serving as secretary with a salary of $1,200 annually.[xxviii]

Many racegoers had criticized the trotting track's location, the size of the grandstand, and the narrowness of the course. As a result, the racing association decided to purchase more than one hundred acres across the street from the old site and to build a new track in time for the 1864 meet.

From the racing association's first meeting came the following announcement in the September 5, 1863, *Wilkes' Spirit of the Times*: "We learn that there is an additional sum of ten thousand dollars to be raised to enable the committee to make all the improvements they may deem necessary. The course is to be of an oval form, after the diagram printed in our Turf Register of 1861 …"[xxix]

Morrissey's trotting rival and friend, Cornelius Vanderbilt, backed Morrissey in his call for subscriptions in establishing a jockey club, which came to be called the Saratoga Association. Vanderbilt offered to put up the entire $10,000, but gave just $3,000 when it was decided to keep membership in the association open to others. In a matter of hours, however, Morrissey had raised $10,600.[xxx] Another $10,000 was raised in subscriptions, and 125 acres across Union Avenue from the old Saratoga Trotting Course were purchased for the new track with funds contributed by Morrissey, Travers, Hunter, and Jerome.

Just three months after the funds were raised, *Wilkes' Spirit of the Times* noted that work on the new track was progressing well. The report stated that the grandstand was completed and indicated that the course was already fenced and the track laid out and graded. It also described the construction: "The new course is on the opposite side of the road from the old course, and close to it. The surface is so nearly level that the eye cannot detect any elevation, though there is, in fact, a very slight rise about the middle of the stretches. These are each 1,360 feet in length, forty feet over a quarter of a mile, the curves round the ends are regular, and the outside of the track on them is thrown up two feet and a half."[xxxi]

With the steady progress on the new course, an ad was posted in the December 19, 1863, issue of *Wilkes' Spirit of the Times* for four days of racing in 1864. The ad notified interested Turfmen that the races would begin with the Travers Stakes, for three-year-olds, with an entrance fee of $50 and an extra $1,000 added.[xxxii]

CHAPTER 4

Norfolk and Kentucky

In June 1864, a couple of months before Saratoga's second meet, Thoroughbred racing's top horses gathered at the Paterson, New Jersey, track for its schedule of high-class races. Among the horses the crowds lined up to see were the brilliant three-year-old colts Norfolk and Kentucky. Both were entered in the June 7 Jersey Derby, a mile-heat race worth $1,000.

Kentucky, a son of Lexington out of the Glencoe mare Magnolia, was owned by John Hunter in partnership with William Travers and George Osgood. The men had acquired Kentucky from his breeder, John Clay, a few months before. Considered the top runner in the East, the colt had excelled as a two-year-old, decisively defeating two other prominent two-year-olds, James Watson's Minnie Minor and J.P. Ackerman's Eagle.

Bred by R.A. Alexander, Norfolk was also by Lexington out of Novice, by Glencoe, and was generally considered the best horse in the race because of his bloodlines and his most recent performance at St. Louis. In the sweepstakes there for three-year-olds in mile heats, Norfolk had taken a cursory tour of the course before claiming it as his own.

"After bolting in each heat, and running around the course alone at St. Louis, he won in such gallant style and excellent time (1 min. 46 1/4 sec., the first heat), that he was forthwith purchased

Norfolk

for $15,001," according to *Wilkes' Spirit of the Times*.[i]

His time for the first heat was an incredible achievement given his warm-up lap and was still just seconds off the American record set by Mammoma at Lexington, Kentucky, in May 1862.

After Norfolk's effort in St. Louis, a spectator was so impressed with the colt's performance that he approached Alexander with an offer to buy the animal. Alexander told the man, Californian Theodore Winters, Norfolk could be purchased on the condition the price exceed what Alexander had paid for the colt's acclaimed sire Lexington.

Winters agreed to Alexander's terms and bought Norfolk for $1 more than Alexander had paid for Lexington.

Nicknamed "Black T"[ii] because of a substantial moustache, Winters was born near Chicago then later moved to Sacramento, California, where he became very wealthy with holdings in gold-mining stock.

At the time of the purchase, rumors abounded that Winters, who maintained residences in Yolo County, California, near the present-day site of the University of California, Davis; and in Washoe County, Nevada, had purchased Norfolk to defeat Lodi, the dominant colt on the West Coast. Owned by one of Winters' business and political rivals, Judge C.H. Bryan, Lodi had defeated Winters' expensive Lexington-sired mare Margaretta.[iii]

Before any match between Norfolk and Lodi could come about, however, Norfolk was scheduled to face Kentucky and other stiff competition in the Jersey Derby, a race that included Zeb Ward's big bay colt Tipperary (about 16 hands compared with the diminutive Norfolk who stood about 15.2 hands).

Sired by Ringgold, Tipperary was considered a legitimate threat to Norfolk, particularly with Abe Hawkins in the irons again. In the sweepstakes for three-year-olds at St. Louis on May 16, Norfolk had distanced most of the field. Only Tipperary had stayed with Norfolk and forced him to run hard and to "stretch his neck"[iv] to win.

The report on the race in the *Wilkes' Spirit of the Times* included this note, "It is not to be forgotten that Tipperary had Abe on his back in this race, and they say that there never was such an amount of cunning, skill, and experience in such a small compass before."[v]

Several days later, again at St. Louis, Tipperary showed his race against Norfolk was no fluke and battled tenaciously against Asteroid, another well-regarded Alexander colt sired by Lexington.

The horses' arrivals at Paterson for the Jersey Derby also coincided with the appearance there of a well-known harness horsemen-turned-gambler — James Eoff.

George Wilkes of *Wilkes' Spirit of the Times* painted a vivid scene: "There was commotion and dismay among the betting fraternity. Up to the day that Norfolk arrived at Paterson there had been no unusual excitement among the speculators in regard to their investments. But soon after this famous colt was comfortably stabled at the course, under the care of his trainer, Ansel, there descended upon this devoted city, much as Lucifer alighted in Paradise, after having swept around the world in cloud and darkness, one James E. (sic) Eoff."[vi]

James Eoff had established a reputation as a successful driver of several prominent trotters and as an authority on horses and horse racing, but his character drew question.

In 1859 Eoff was the owner and trainer of the acclaimed trotter Princess, who had a series of spirited duels with the renowned trotter Flora Temple. On June 22 that year, the *New York Times* reported on one of their matches and the ensuing controversy that almost caused Eoff to be ruled off the Eclipse Course.

The race had been staged the previous week and had generated so much controversy that Eoff was compelled to face the Union Jockey Club (under whose auspices the trot was held). The hearing was held to investigate whether "the California mare Princess had not justice done her by her driver."[vii] After providing Eoff the opportunity to make his own statement, club officials listened to more than two hours of testimony denouncing Eoff.

Eoff managed to avoid the punishment in this particular instance when he offered to provide another race against Flora Temple, but that the hearing was held at all and brought forth such an animated response indicates his peers greatly questioned Eoff's professional conduct.

Neither was it the last time that Eoff's professional conduct was considered questionable. In a subsequent race between Princess and Flora Temple, officials again questioned Eoff afterward. In the August 25, 1859, report of the *New York Times*, the reporter wrote, "It seemed to be the general opinion that Princess was badly driven — that she could do much better if rightly handled, though it is probably certain that Flora would always have the advantage in trotting on a half-mile track as Princess is much more apt to 'break' on the turns. Mr. Eoff stated that he did not expect to win the race when he came on the course, and had so stated to his friends in the morning. He was severely censured by those who knew of it, for coming upon the Judges' stands during the race."[viii]

Still, Eoff generally was acknowledged as an authority on racing by his peers and later would return to a successful career as an owner and trainer of trotters. At the time of the 1864 meeting at Saratoga, however, Eoff had decided to augment his income with gambling on Thoroughbred racing.

When he arrived at Paterson, he immediately began to visit the gaming houses on upper and lower Broadway and ingratiated himself with other gamblers. *Wilkes' Spirit of the Times* reported, "Eoff began to oscillate about in pendulum style between the upper and lower gaming-houses in Broadway, and being gifted with a prolific invention and an amount of plausibility and brass that would have cheated the devil himself, had he been in the situation of Dr. Faust of Tom Walker, he soon inflated diverse persons with the notion that now was the time to make much money."[ix]

In his conversations at the gaming houses, Eoff implied he was involved in management and control of Norfolk. He also was later accused of telling other gamblers that unless he was allowed to organize some gambling pools on the Jersey Derby with bets on Norfolk "against Captain Moore's entry,"[x] Norfolk would not be allowed to start.

Then Eoff managed to convince other gamblers that Norfolk was unfit and that he had the power to prevent Norfolk from starting in the Jersey Derby. Eoff implied if his demands were not met, Norfolk would actually skip the Jersey Derby and be shipped to California.

Norfolk's main rival, Kentucky

It was a particularly convenient time for Eoff to target bets regarding Norfolk with wild accusations and rumors because as Eoff pointed out in his letter to *Wilkes' Spirit of the Times*, "Mr. Winters was in the Convention at Baltimore, as a delegate from California."[xi]

Eoff's story was so convincing that soon after his arrival, investors in the various pools began to back away from Norfolk for the upcoming meet. Instead gamblers shifted their money to what was considered a safer bet, Captain T.G. Moore's bay colt by Lexington out of Gloriana, by American Eclipse, because the other nominal favorite, Kentucky, did not appear to be in racing form. *Wilkes' Spirit of the Times* reported, "Kentucky was much admired, and with perfect justice, for he is a splendid colt. But there was an apparent lack of hard polish about him, which is fully accounted for by the fact that that his work was stopped twice toward the close of his preparation."[xii]

With rumors swirling about Norfolk's status, even John

Morrissey, always on the trail of the action, was drawn into the controversy with Eoff about Norfolk. Morrissey, a professional gambler, put up $2,000 to $6,000 that Norfolk would not win, as Eoff admitted later. He wrote, "... and I bet Mr. Morrissey two thousand to six thousand that Norfolk would win, and bet him [Morrissey] that he would start. Mr. Morrissey says Norfolk would not have started, if he had not made these bets."[xiii]

With Morrissey's money already committed, Eoff somehow managed to convince Morrissey to bet against him that Norfolk would not even start. Despite Eoff's persuasive stories, as the races were about to begin Norfolk again became the heavy favorite among local bettors. Morrissey then realized that he had been duped by the scheming Eoff and was furious. *Wilkes' Spirit of the Times* noted, "The roars of the enraged 'tiger' when he found himself enmeshed, and felt the preparatory tickling of the spear through the cords of the net, shook the very earth at Paterson."[xiv]

Undoubtedly, Morrissey was furious he had been outwitted in a gambling scheme, but Morrissey also probably realized he was in no position to confront Eoff personally or avenge himself. He was in the process of becoming a successful businessman who depended on the genteel classes for his income and could ill afford a press report of public brawling.

On race day a field of twelve colts and fillies lined up for the Jersey Derby, including Kentucky, Tipperary, and the much-speculated-upon Norfolk. Despite all the scheming and rumors, Norfolk appeared at the starting line, apparently in good racing condition. Later Eoff seemed to imply that Winters was in on the scheme when the gambler admitted in his note that the owner never even considered not starting the colt.[xv]

In fact, Norfolk continued to dominate the three-year-old class by winning the race. He broke away from the pack right at the start and was never challenged. The report in *Wilkes' Spirit of the Times* summarized that the start seemed to end the race as soon as it began, "The favorite had the advantage, and being able to go like a bullet from the jump he was lengths away, while the others were all tangled up, Tip among them."[xvi]

Kentucky broke away next from the pack but was unable to match the torrid pace that Norfolk set, and Tipperary was unable to break away from the pack until late in the race and then could not close up with the front-running Norfolk.

Norfolk's winning time was 1:47.[xvii] Tipperary finished second, ahead of Eagle, and Kentucky was a disappointing fourth.

For his scheming, Eoff made as much as $20,000 that day,[xviii] and it was rumored that Norfolk's new owner, Winters, walked away with as much as $100,000 from the betting pools.[xix] If true, it would indicate that, in fact, Eoff and Winters had colluded, but the investigation indicated that Eoff had teamed up with one of Winters' hired men, Charles Marsh.

After the race, the executive committee of the Passaic County Agricultural Association, which ran the Paterson race meetings, met to discuss the rumors that had swirled about Norfolk. Eoff was called to testify. Based on his testimony and evidence never released to the public, the committee found "collusion and fraud in relation to the running of the colt Norfolk in the Jersey Derby, perpetrated by James L. Eoff, with the knowledge or collusion of Charles Marsh."[xx]

Eoff was ruled off the Paterson track forever, and Marsh was censured. Finally, the committee ruled that Norfolk was suspended from racing on the Paterson track until further notice.

If the shadowy con artist hadn't successfully singled out Morrissey for his scam at the Paterson races, there might still have been a chance that Norfolk could have run at Saratoga. But because Morrissey had been duped to the tune of somewhere between $5,000 and $7,000[xxi] by the slippery gambler, that opportunity was lost.

In the wake of the executive committee's decision, and no doubt Morrissey's injured pride, the Saratoga managers (which meant Morrissey and Wheatly) quickly decided to dismiss Norfolk's entries for the races at the upcoming Saratoga meet. Winters promptly put Norfolk on a boat for San Francisco.

As Winters and Norfolk sailed for the West Coast, where the horseman also planned to use Norfolk to establish a stud farm in Yolo County, other owners and horses gathered for the second year of racing at Saratoga.

Kentucky and Tipperary were both expected to run in the inaugural Travers Stakes — named for Saratoga Racing Association president William Travers — but Norfolk's absence prevented Saratoga patrons from seeing a rubber match between Norfolk and Kentucky to determine the year's best three-year-old.

On opening day, August 2, 1864, five horses lined up to contest the Travers, a mile-and-three-quarters sweepstakes with a purse of $2,500. Tipperary emerged as the favorite in the betting pools. Kentucky also had extensive backing, as would be expected. At the Paterson meet, Kentucky had followed his fourth-place finish in the Jersey Derby with a score in the two-mile Sequel Stakes, a race in which Norfolk had been scratched due to the Eoff controversy. But Kentucky had recently been dealing with a navicular bone injury, and no one could be sure that he would even race.

Abe Hawkins again was aboard Tipperary but was not nearly as confident as he had been at Paterson when his horse was healthy. Tipperary had developed an enlarged curb on a hock,[xxii] which had forced a reduction in his workouts, and as a result Tipperary was struggling to remain in peak shape.

As the horses and owners gathered for the meeting, there was a general consensus on the new course and grandstand. "From all that we have heard, the new course is one of the best ever constructed in America," reported *Wilkes' Spirit of the Times*. [xxiii] "The site, soil and work done on it are such as to make it fast and safe ... The Grand Stand is two hundred feet long, and so admirably devised and constructed that from every seat on it the running horses can be seen in every part of their swift career."[xxiv]

A large crowd turned out for the inaugural running of the Travers Stakes, which was already clearly regarded as an "event." Wilkes reported, "When the bell rang for the saddling of the horses in the Travers Stake, we estimated the number of people on the ground at five thousand. The greater part of these were ladies richly and elegantly attired ... The present style of 'jockey-hat,' with its jaunty plumes and gay ribbons, just suits the race-course, and the superb toilets which the ladies had put on to do honor to this occasion, could hardly be surpassed for splendor and good taste."[xxv]

Without Norfolk eligible to start at Saratoga, the field suffered greatly. He had been the class of the three-year-olds that season with his victories at St. Louis and Paterson. With the status of Kentucky still undecided, Tipperary became the favorite in the pools. When the contenders were brought onto the course, it was noticed that Kentucky was already "well warmed up."[xxvi] It was learned later that Kentucky's trainer, A.J. Minor, had already run Kentucky for three or four miles on the old course to make sure his "lameness"[xxvii] would not prevent him from running well.

Five horses went to the start: Kentucky, Tipperary, Patti, Ringmaster, and a gray colt by Eclipse. The colts carried one hundred pounds and the filly, ninety-seven. At the start the filly, Patti, took the lead with Frances Morris' gray colt by Eclipse close behind. Following behind them was Kentucky with Tipperary close to him and Ringmaster last. The horses kept this order until they ran past the grandstand, and as they came out of the turn, Kentucky and Tipperary passed the gray colt and Patti, with Ringmaster falling far behind.

On the backstretch Kentucky had a slight lead on Tipperary, followed by the gray Eclipse colt, Patti, and Ringmaster. As Kentucky came out of the final turn, he increased his lead by three or four lengths on Tipperary and was in control of the race. With an almost overwhelming lead, Gilbert "Gilpatrick" Patrick reined Kentucky in and he cantered to the finish in a time of 3:18 2/4. Kentucky finished three lengths ahead of Tipperary, followed by the gray colt, Patti, and Ringmaster.

Two days later Kentucky and Tipperary met again in a two-mile event for three-year-olds, worth $1,750. As a result of his Travers win, Kentucky was required to carry five more pounds than his three opponents (105 to 100). Morris' gray Eclipse colt showed up for another round, with a new starter in Orion, a good-looking bay son of Revenue.

Kentucky, a 2-1 favorite among the bettors, had the inside post position. Orion was next, followed by the gray colt, and Tipperary on the outside. After the break Tipperary took the lead with Orion second, Kentucky third, and the gray colt last. Down the backstretch Orion took a slight lead, as Kentucky passed Tipperary and moved into second. As the horses approached the grandstand, Kentucky passed Orion to gain the lead. Tipperary continued in third, followed by the gray colt. As the field began the second mile, Kentucky opened a two-length lead, but it was clear from the stands that Gilpatrick was not yet letting his horse run full out. Tipperary moved into second, followed by Orion, and the gray. In the homestretch Kentucky opened up a three-length lead and won easily, followed by Tipperary, Orion, and the gray colt. The two-mile time was 4:11 3/4.

Kentucky seemed to have confirmed his status as the country's top three-year-old with his decisive victories at Saratoga, even with Norfolk's absence.

On the final day of the meet, a mile-heat race was carded for three-year-olds that had been winless at Paterson and Saratoga, and Tipperary was the heavy favorite. While the race was for beaten horses, it was still an important race for Tipperary and his supporters, who had entered the season and meeting with great expectations. In fact, during the season Tipperary had raced well; he just hadn't been able to defeat the Lexington-sired horses in five attempts. Twice he had finished second to Norfolk, once to Asteroid, and twice to Kentucky. Still, rumors spread quickly that if Tipperary could not win this race, his owner would rest him until the next season.

With Tipperary still considered the dominant horse despite his losses, most of the betting was on which horse would finish second, and a great deal of money was invested in Patti and Orion.

Tipperary won the first heat easily in a time of 1:59, with the Eclipse filly second, Orion third, and Patti last. In the second heat Tipperary took the lead, was never headed, and won in 2:02.

As the races in Saratoga finished for the 1864 season, Norfolk, the blackballed top-flight runner who had been involved in the Paterson scandal, was still en route to San Francisco, from where he would be transferred to Winters' Rancho del Arroyo in Yolo County.

As for the man who laid a trap and ensnared John Morrissey with his well-laid plans, James Eoff refused to slink away before responding to his suspension at Paterson. In a letter addressed to *Wilkes' Spirit of the Times* and published in the June 18 issue, Eoff denied any wrongdoing and managed to blame Morrissey for his plight:

> You will see by the report of this day's racing that I have been ruled off the Paterson track, and also Mr. Winters'

colt Norfolk, the winner of yesterday's Derby ... I am not a member of the Paterson Association, own no horse, entered no horse, control no horse, infringed on no rules of said track — am an outsider entirely. I leave it to the patrons of the turf to say if I have been treated right ...

I cannot see what Mr. Winter's (sic) horse Norfolk has done that he should be ruled off and not allowed to start for the Sequel stake to-morrow, unless it is to favor some leather-flapper that is not worthy of the name of race-horse to win the Sequel stake tomorrow; or whether they took Mr. Morrissey's opinion that I [Eoff] was in some way able to control Norfolk's starting or not starting ...[xxviii]

In that same letter Eoff clearly showed great pleasure in making a fool of Morrissey and taking his money:

"Mr. Morrissey probably knows that he has been beaten out of his money and I guess that is all he knows, only that he has had me and Norfolk, the best race-horse he ever saw, ruled off without any cause, only feeling."[xxix]

With that said, Eoff appears to have taken his ill-gotten gains and exited from the Thoroughbred racing scene. He later resumed his career as a driver for trotters and harness racers, an occupation for which he had some talent and success. Eoff was no stranger to the winner's circle, and in 1866 he managed to purchase a prominent contemporary trotter, General Butler.

His adversary and foil, Morrissey, had proven capable as manager of the Saratoga track and under his guidance it grew and prospered. The racing season had been extended, and purses were significantly larger. Five years after the races opened in 1863, Saratoga was still the only racetrack that featured Thoroughbred racing in August.

With the track proving a success, John and Susie Morrissey reveled in the limelight. Visitors frequently asked where they would be most likely to catch a glimpse of the elegant and striking Susie Morrissey, who was always stylishly dressed.

John Morrissey himself often could be found attired in elegant evening dress at the gate leading to the casino in Congress Park. A striking figure, Morrissey often dressed in a tall beaver hat, a swallow-tailed coat, striped trousers, patent leather boots, and white kid gloves with a $5,000 diamond on his shirt and smaller diamonds in his cuff links. He would mingle with the well-heeled crowd at his casino, a crowd that included millionaires, tycoons, industrial titans, a president's son, and, later, a former president, congressmen and senators, generals, artists and musicians, and women adorned with fabulous jewels and resplendent gowns.

◆◆◆◆

By 1875, Saratoga Race Course had garnered enough prestige to draw regularly the finest horses, and the races served as a focal point for summer entertainment, drawing some of America's most prominent names.

If success is measured in emulation, the racetrack at Saratoga had become very successful. Since the first races at the new Saratoga oval in 1864, the track had served as a model and/ or inspiration for several other new racecourses in the New York area, including Jerome Park, which opened in 1867, and Monmouth Park, near Long Branch, New Jersey, which opened in 1870.

The winner of the first Travers, Kentucky, would go on to a remarkable career in which the only race he lost had been that against Norfolk, at Paterson. Among his wins were two consecutive victories in the Saratoga Cup, which began in 1865 before a crowd of 10,000.[xxx]

Four years later, in 1869, August Belmont, the wealthy banker and chairman of the Democratic Party, appeared with Glenelg, who won the Travers that season. Glenelg was high strung as a two-year-old and grew to a well-muscled 16 hands with a seventy-two-inch girth. After retirement Glenelg would become the U.S. champion sire four times.[xxxi]

By 1875, the cream of the horse crop appeared at Saratoga as a matter of course, often leading to championship-caliber match-ups. One of these was the 1875 Saratoga Cup featuring Springbok and Preakness, but that particular race involved much more than just the horses.

CHAPTER 5

Doing the Most Good

For several months, racing fans had eagerly anticipated the two-and-a-quarter-mile Saratoga Cup. The morning of July 29, 1875, patrons began arriving on the early train, and just moments from first post, the road to the track was still jammed, the footways clogged with pedestrians. The growing crowd took almost two hours to settle in.

The half-mile Flash Stakes for two-year-olds opened the day's racing on an ominous note. As the colts and fillies were brought to the starting line for the half-mile dash, there were repeated false starts. Finally, the nervous race officials ordered that the horses be forced to walk in a circle to settle down. Some of the juveniles were so agitated, however, they could not be calmed.

Despite the pre-race commotion, all went well at the start. When the horses approached the homestretch, however, David McDaniel's unnamed chestnut filly slipped past Lewis and Company's Lady Clipper. Behind McDaniel's filly the rest of the field was bunched together, and in the struggle for second place, Lady Clipper was knocked down, throwing her jockey headfirst several feet. Then Lawrence and Lorillard's Warlock stumbled over the fallen filly, sending his jockey into a hard fall.

Fortunately, Lady Clipper's jockey was able to walk away

unscathed, but Warlock's jockey lay sprawled and motionless on the track for several frightening moments before finally getting up. Although Lorillard's filly Faithless won the race by six lengths, a claim for foul riding was later lodged against Faithless' jockey. However, it was disallowed.

Oblivious to the near-life-and-death drama unfolding on the track, the large crowd continued to filter in for the feature race. The betting for the Saratoga Cup was said to be unprecedented as nearly a half-million dollars changed hands among the eager fans and spectators.[i] The betting public favored David McDaniel's Springbok. In one pool that totaled $5,925, $2,000 was wagered on Springbok; $1,400 on Henry Price McGrath's Aaron Pennington; $1,250 on Thomas Puryear's entry of Grinstead and Rutherford; $600 on August Belmont's Olitipa; $325 on Mark A. Littel's Wild Idle; and $300 on Milton H. Sanford's Preakness.[ii]

Even up until post time, the pool managers continued to receive telegrams from out-of-town parties anxious that their money be placed "where it would do the most good."[iii] The feverish betting spawned a rumor around the track that an alarmed John Morrissey, the track's owner and manager, had demanded betting pools be closed. Despite the rumor that Morrissey had enforced a closing of the pools, Henry Price McGrath, Morrissey's former gambling partner and the founder of McGrathiana Stud in Kentucky, casually picked a spot, elevated himself above the milling fans and gamblers, and then boldly announced he had a "few remarks"[iv] for the crowd.

A large man who moved with an easy self-assurance, McGrath usually wore a white coat with a bright red tie, standing out even in a large crowd. Some of the gathering fans at Saratoga may have even recognized him as the owner of Aristides, the horse who earlier that season had won the first Kentucky Derby.

With success seeming his traveling companion, McGrath was

Springbok

comfortable speaking to large crowds and casually announced to the assemblage around him that he had "just received a dispatch from New York to put $250 on Pennington, and I don't want anyone to bid against me."[v]

Although a correspondent from the Chicago *Tribune* had provided a character sketch of the personable McGrath: "... gruff, ... always pleasing, and never insulting or vindictive,"[vi] events that had occurred a couple of weeks earlier in Saratoga had brought out a darker side of the otherwise affable man.

Despite all his betting bravado on that opening day, McGrath was fortunate to be there. A week earlier, McGrath had physically confronted and assaulted George Wilkes, the editor of *Wilkes' Spirit of the Times*, who also owned and raced horses. The attack, provoked by a long-running feud between the men, came to a head at Saratoga's United States Hotel.

Wilkes had just published accusations that McGrath personally profited when his horses repeatedly and unexpectedly lost in big races and called McGrath and his former partner, Johnny

McGrathiana Stud, H.P. McGrath's Kentucky estate

Chamberlin, "the two skin-gamblers who run the Monmouth Race Track"[vii] and "no better than highway robbers."[viii]

After publishing these explosive accusations, Wilkes hastened to Saratoga for the 1875 meeting and registered at the United States Hotel. As fate would have it, McGrath also registered at the same hotel, and it was just a matter of time before the men collided, resulting in McGrath's assault. Bystanders described the attack as a trivial incident with no real physical damage done, and both men walked away unharmed. The principal damage lay in the notoriety that both men acquired for the crime of disrupting the quiet of a genteel Saratoga.

While there was little physical injury to either man, the confrontation exacerbated the hostility between them and resulted in both men suing each other. George Wilkes filed an assault and battery charge against McGrath while McGrath sued Wilkes to recover $25,000 damages for the libelous article titled "The Monmouth Man-Trap," published in the July 17 issue.[ix]

Following the incident at the hotel, on July 22, 1875, one

of McGrath's counsels, Mr. Foley, prepared a legal complaint, and an order of arrest was issued requiring the county sheriff to arrest Wilkes. The warrant, served to Wilkes at the United States Hotel, called for a $1,500 bond. Wilkes attempted to put up the cash to post bond but was unable to find the necessary funds. Only a friend's guarantee that Wilkes would appear in court the following day at 11 a.m. prevented the publisher from landing in jail.

The warrant stipulated, however, that if Wilkes could not by then post bond, he was to be incarcerated at the Ballston jail. That would, of course, preclude his appearing in court at 2:30 p.m. against McGrath, who had been charged with assault and battery stemming from the incident at the hotel.

McGrath also was bound over to authorities for his actions that morning at the hotel and to ensure that there would be no further incidents. In response to the public shaming for inciting a disturbance, McGrath later attempted to justify his actions, explaining he had only accosted Wilkes because he would have been afraid to present himself in his home state had he not attempted to defend himself and his honor.

The long-simmering feud had begun in 1863 when John Morrissey established Thoroughbred racing in Saratoga. Morrissey's immediate and dramatic success at Saratoga encouraged two former partners and professional gamblers, Chamberlin and McGrath, to establish a rival racecourse at Long Branch.

Like Morrissey, McGrath came from a working-class family and had led a colorful life. McGrath had been born in Versailles, Woodford County, Kentucky, in 1813. He was the son of a tailor and had been taught the business as a child. He had been expected to follow his father into the trade. But the young McGrath had other vocational interests and quickly became an adept card player. He learned to play all the most popular card games and was especially adept at poker and a game called "old sledge."[x]

McGrath decided to forego the family business. He struck out on his own and proceeded to lead the unpredictable and often chaotic life of a wandering professional gambler, roaming the West and the South in search of action. In his days as a wandering "sport,"[xi] McGrath came to know many of the old Mississippi River steamboat captains and made some lifelong friendships.

McGrath's travels eventually took him to Vicksburg, Mississippi, where he rubbed elbows with some prominent and influential men, including future Governor Alexander McNutt and future U.S. Congressman Sargent Prentiss. Later, McGrath landed in New Orleans, and in 1832, with a group of professional gamblers, he opened "the finest gambling house in the South."[xii]

While working in the New Orleans gambling den, McGrath envisioned the concept of selling betting pools, and it was there that pool selling originated. The practice at that time had been for McGrath and his colleagues to act as the depository for stakes in the games, for which they charged a commission.

The practice then evolved as the gamblers began to provide receipts and charge a commission when they staked cash for card players. The innovation proved so successful that huge crowds flocked to the gambling house, and the gamblers were forced to issue tickets of invitation and charge a $10 admission fee. Sometime after this practice was implemented, McGrath came up with the idea of selling choices on races, acting as the auctioneer and his partners acting as pool writers.

The ambitious and increasingly successful McGrath decided to leave New Orleans for a bigger market, New York City, where he formed a partnership with Morrissey and Chamberlin. In New York McGrath was known as a heavy bettor and once won

$45,000 in a single game of the popular card game "Boston."[xiii] He helped out Morrissey at the first Saratoga meeting by assigning weights for the horses.

In spring 1864, McGrath returned to Lexington and withdrew $250,000 out of the continuing game in the New York City gambling house where he worked. He purchased five hundred acres of the finest bluegrass land and converted it into a stock farm, which he called McGrathiana.

On that land McGrath built a huge house, where he held extravagant parties for his friends on the Sunday that preceded the spring and fall meetings of the Kentucky Association. He also continued to gamble successfully, and in 1875 when he arrived at Saratoga for the big race, he had already won $50,000.[xiv]

His rival, George Wilkes, was a proud man who had founded his paper devoted to sporting issues in the 1850s. It had become the longest running sporting paper in New York. He bitterly opposed the entry of gambling professionals in Thoroughbred racing, and the success of professional gamblers at Saratoga and Long Branch prompted accusations of foul play.

In his "The Monmouth Man-Trap"[xv] article, Wilkes made clear he personally liked McGrath but deeply resented the intrusion of a professional gambler into the business and sport of horseracing. Of McGrath, Wilkes wrote, "He is gifted with a rank wit, but has a good nature."[xvi]

In the article Wilkes also made his point about the inherent conflict in allowing a professional gambler such as McGrath to ply his trade in horseracing. Wilkes wrote, "But, though he tells good stories and is very liberal with his liquor, he remains only a skin-gambler after all, and, despite of his many virtues, he tickles those snap-roulettes against his customer, and remains the co-partner of the rascal Chamberlin. Anyone who supposes that men of these pursuits would not *throw* a race, or enter horses like Tom Ochiltree, for the purpose of losing, know but little of human nature."[xvii]

Wilkes then accused McGrath, with the best stable in America at the time, of running his horses successfully for much of the racing season, to gain the backing of the betting public and then abusing that public trust for personal profit when he arranged for his horses to lose in big races.

In private and in his columns, Wilkes maintained that in a race the week before the Saratoga Cup, the Derby winner, Aristides, had been watered to excess to ensure that he couldn't win and that McGrath had won enormous sums of money from private bets on the race.

Wilkes wrote that McGrath's acclaimed horse Tom Bowling also was weighted with water in the 1873 Ocean Hotel Stakes to ensure he couldn't win, allowing a relatively unknown horse, Lizzie Lucas, to prevail. He wrote, "It will be recollected that the amount of money which was laid upon Tom Bowling, on the occasion of 1873, was enormous, it being wagered, in consequence of his transcendent merits, at an odds of 3 to 1, but to the surprise of everybody, and to the utter dismay of his backers, he performed most ingloriously in the race (though McGrath pretended to support him till the last moment), and the immense plunder was consequently transferred to the holders of the cheap pool tickets, bought by the sly investors upon Lizzie Lucas."[xviii]

Wilkes also alleged that Tom Bowling had been given an unfair advantage with a "flying start" in a recent race on Johnny Chamberlin's Long Branch course.[xix]

The continuing onslaught of accusations and simmering resentments finally provoked a response from Chamberlin, who ordered the "free badge"[xx] torn off Wilkes' reporter at Long Branch. Soon afterward, Wilkes retaliated and published a series of "domestic, personal, and fierce"[xxi] articles on Chamberlin and his management of the Long Branch course.

Chamberlin then sought an indictment for libel against Wilkes. While nothing ever came of this, hard feelings continued to fester between the professional gamblers and the publisher.

The Chicago *Tribune* correspondent who reported on the feud noted that most racing professionals did not support Wilkes' accusations. The correspondent reported that McGrath was well liked by his peers and wrote that McGrath was actually considered "the very soul of honor."[xxii]

Still, some people found the allegations very troubling. Wealthy racing enthusiasts such as August Belmont, George and Pierre Lorillard, and Milton Sanford had invested a great deal of time, energy, and large sums of money to improve the Thoroughbred stock of the country and to elevate Thoroughbred racing as a sport. These men also tended to gamble heavily on their horses in the races, and in return they demanded that the races be free of any taint of manipulation or corruption.

It is easy to believe that men such as these also shared Wilkes' resentment of the intrusion by outsiders into their beloved sport. Belmont had bluntly characterized his feelings after the construction of Jerome Park, when he said "racing is for the rich."[xxiii]

In fact, it is hard to imagine that wealthy and powerful men such as the Lorillards, Sanford, and Belmont could not have deeply resented the influence and success of outsiders and professional gamblers such as Morrissey, Chamberlin, and McGrath, both for professional and personal reasons.

The significance of this feud cannot be measured merely by the personal fortunes of Wilkes and McGrath. The feud also had important implications for the viability and popularity of the sport, and the correspondent for the Chicago *Tribune* depicted in his article of August 1, 1875, the increasingly bitter hostility that alienated Turf professionals and owners.

The personal feud between Wilkes and McGrath, the

correspondent wrote, was actually a sign of the growing rivalry between two socioeconomic groups vying for supremacy in the increasingly popular sport. Racing's old guard, corporate tycoons and the very wealthy, had come to resent the intrusion of men such as McGrath and other professional gamblers who were successfully transitioning to racetrack management and Thoroughbred ownership. The correspondent wrote, "It is the issue between professional gaming men and the rich amateurs of the turf that is incidentally to be pressed on this fight wherein is consequence."[xxiv]

The continuing struggle for lucrative prize money, the pride of ownership between professional gaming men and the rich amateurs, and control of the sport all seemed to intersect that day in July for the honor of winning the 1875 Saratoga Cup.

Representing the group of wealthy Thoroughbred owners who were instrumental in creating and maintaining championship-caliber racing in America were Milton H. Sanford and August Belmont. They had the resources to buy the best horses and to provide them with the finest training facilities. For their investments, they expected to win.

Belmont was a wealthy financier and the leader of a clique of very affluent and influential men who considered horse racing their pride and passion. He owned a successful Long Island stable that had included several championship caliber Thoroughbreds including Glenelg, winner of the 1869 Travers, and Kingfisher, who had won the Belmont Stakes in 1870.

Belmont's entry this day was Olitipa, a three-year-old bright chestnut filly with white legs. Sired by Leamington and out of Oliata, Olitipa, as a juvenile, had won the Nursery Stakes and the half-mile Flash Stakes at Saratoga, where she had set a new record of :47 3/4. Her successes also included the Ladies' Maryland Stakes, Hunter Stakes, and the one-and-a-quarter-mile Alabama Stakes. The lone filly in the Saratoga Cup field,

Olitipa was asked to carry a shade less than ninety pounds.

Milton Sanford was the son of a cotton-thread-mill owner, Samuel Sanford, and inherited his father's business. Sanford then made a fortune providing blankets for the war effort during the Civil War and became one of New England's wealthiest men.

In addition to his talent for making money, Sanford loved fast horses and used his fortune to build a prominent racing stable. He established a training farm for his horses near Paterson, New Jersey, where a racetrack was opened in 1864. Sanford built three stables with forty-two stalls, a blacksmith shop, a training ring, and a three-quarters-mile training track. To ensure that his horses were competitive with any other stable in America, Sanford hired a talented young Englishman, William Hayward, to act as the trainer and jockey. The farm was called Preakness Farms after an old Indian name.

Unlike Belmont and Sanford, McGrath was neither independently wealthy nor part of the elite East Coast social set. Only with perseverance, hard work, and some favorable fortune had McGrath managed to create a good life for himself. On that day at Saratoga, when Price McGrath finished soliciting the crowd for support in the pools for his horse Aaron Pennington, he also crossed social and financial boundaries that had once been unassailable when he walked onto the course at Saratoga to compete with Belmont and Sanford.

The Saratoga Cup combined a potentially large stake value and prestige and had originally enticed a quality field of twenty-three nominations.

In addition, an important change to the race's conditions that year had increased the incentive for owners: Stake money was offered in place of the traditional Saratoga Cup. The winner's share would be worth the entrance money of $2,150, plus the value of the cup stake, which could be significant.

Despite the potentially significant purse, when the horses finally lined up for the race, there had already been significant withdrawals, including David McDaniel's Acrobat, who had finished in a near dead heat with Pierre Lorillard's Attila in the 1874 Travers. Just months before the Saratoga Cup. Acrobat had been the decided favorite in the pools, but his most recent performances were not promising and his trainer judged him unfit for the race.

Still, McDaniel had good reason to be optimistic about his chances. Like McGrath, McDaniel was an outsider from the South (he owned land in North Carolina) with a questionable background as an ex-slave dealer.[xxv] His entrée into Saratoga racing was paved by a string of very successful years as an owner and trainer between 1870 and 1874.

McDaniel had owned and trained Harry Bassett, Joe Daniels, and Springbok, all of whom had made their marks on racing in that period.

As race time neared, the seven horses that actually showed at the starting line included McDaniel's Springbok. McDaniel probably felt confident that his Springbok was the class of the race, as he had been when he won it in 1874. Many track veterans also considered the 16-hand, bright chestnut Springbok as the horse to watch in the race.

Sired by Australian out of Hester, by Lexington, the five-year-old Springbok was bred by A.J. Alexander and became one of the pre-eminent runners of the day. In 1873 Springbok won the one-and-five-eighths-mile Belmont Stakes, finished second in the two-mile Jerome Handicap, and ran third in the two-mile Kenner Stakes. In the 1874 Saratoga Cup, Springbok easily defeated the aging but game Preakness by several lengths. For his efforts Springbok was unofficially regarded as the year's American champion older male, an honor signifying the best horse of the year.

Olitipa

Despite all of Springbok's accomplishments and talent, winning the Saratoga Cup on this day, even with the accomplished jockey Billy Clark on top, would be no easy feat.

McGrath's Aaron Pennington and Thomas Puryear's Grinstead, both carrying 108 pounds, were considered viable contenders.

Aaron Pennington, a four-year-old bay colt by Tipperary out of Lucy Fowler, by Albion, had been running very well for two successive seasons, including a third in the 1974 Belmont Stakes.

Thomas Puryear and Company's four-year-old bay horse Grinstead, sired by Gilroy out of Sister to Ruric, by Sovereign, also had several strong races to his credit. He had won the six-furlong Champagne Stakes in 1873 and finished second in the 1874 Belmont Stakes behind Saxon. Puryear also was represented in the Saratoga Cup by the four-year-old chestnut horse Rutherford (by Australian out of Aerolite), who also carried 108 pounds.

Also going to the post was Mark A. Littel's five-year-old bay horse Wild Idle, by Australian out of the champion race mare Idlewild, a former holder of the American record for three miles. Wild Idle had two victories to his credit, the Fordham Handicap and the Jockey Club Handicap at Jerome Park, and had already finished in front of Rutherford in a four-mile race. He was saddled with the co-top weight of 114 pounds.

Despite the intense competition McGrath expected Aaron Pennington would prevail. Some of the best racers of the day were included in his stable: Endorser, Rhynodine, Calvin, Bob Wooly, Leonard, Tom Bowling, and the Derby winner, Aristides. Because of the quality of the McGrath runners, his entries were often prime contenders, and when McGrath believed one of his horses would win, he was known to support it unabashedly. When confident of victory, McGrath pushed to have his horses posted as the favorite and backed them heavily and openly.

Rounding out the field was Sanford's eight-year-old bay Preakness, who shared top weight. Sired by Lexington out of Bay Leaf, by Yorkshire, Preakness was considered little more than an afterthought in this field of younger horses. Preakness was a quality runner, but many track observers considered him past his prime.

Preakness was a large horse, standing more than 16 hands high. As a four-year-old, Preakness won two prestigious races at Jerome Park, the Westchester Cup in which he defeated Glenelg, and the Maturity Stakes. But at the age of five, Preakness suffered a setback when he sustained a serious loin injury. Although never quite the same after his injury, the game old Preakness continued to race competitively and occasionally flashed the form that had made him an outstanding runner, as when he won the Jockey Club Handicap at age six.

As the horses moved onto the track, Springbok, who also carried 114 pounds, led the pools with Aaron Pennington the second choice and Rutherford third. The start was clean, and both Springbok and Preakness, with Billy Hayward up, jumped into the lead with Olitipa, ridden by Mr. Sparling, close behind.

At the furlong pole it was Rutherford, with Mr. Donahue up, who had shot into first with a "sizzling"[xxvi] pace, followed by Preakness, Olitipa, and Wild Idle, with N. Heywood up. The pace increased noticeably when Wild Idle moved to challenge Rutherford for the lead at the grandstand.

Rutherford maintained a half-length lead on Wild Idle as they passed the stand, finishing the first quarter-mile in :26 1/4. Next came Springbok, who had a length on Preakness, who was followed by Olitipa, Aaron Pennington, with Mr. Swim up, and Grinstead, with George Barbee up.

As they came out of the turn, Wild Idle lunged past.Rutherford into the lead. Rutherford still had three lengths on Preakness, followed by Springbok and Aaron Pennington while Olitipa and Grinstead fought it out over sixth place.

Going into the backstretch, Wild Idle opened a gap of three lengths on Rutherford, who was two lengths ahead of Preakness. Four lengths back was Springbok, who had a short lead on Aaron Pennington. Olitipa was next and Grinstead was again alone in seventh place, appearing to be biding his time.

At the half-mile pole Wild Idle still led by three over Rutherford, with a time of :52 1/2. Three lengths back, Preakness was still in third, two lengths ahead of Springbok. Aaron Pennington was a half-length back and a length in front of Grinstead, who had now pulled slightly ahead of Olitipa.

Nothing changed in the order as the horses rounded the far turn, but when they headed into the homestretch, the surging Preakness pulled even with Rutherford and then at the furlong pole moved ahead into second. As they made their second pass in front of the grandstand, having finished the first mile and a quarter of the race, Wild Idle was still in first place, with a time

Preakness

of 2:12 1/4. But Preakness continued to gain on Wild Idle and when they passed the stand, he was just a half-length behind.

While Wild Idle and Preakness fought for first place, Rutherford refused to quit and stayed close to the leaders, a neck behind Preakness. Four lengths back was Aaron Pennington, a half-length in front of Springbok, who had a length on Olitipa, with Grinstead again falling back into seventh place. As they came around the turn, Springbok finally unleashed his run, passing Aaron Pennington and approaching Rutherford's head.

Down the backstretch the race tightened considerably. Wild Idle and Preakness battled for the lead. Then Preakness pulled into first just as Springbok passed the faltering Rutherford. Springbok's hold on second place was short-lived as a charging Aaron Pennington passed him. Aaron Pennington and Springbok traded places several times before Springbok again moved ahead.

At the half-mile pole Preakness was just a length ahead of Springbok, who in turn was a length ahead of Aaron Pennington, followed by Wild Idle, a half-length back. As they came around the lower turn, it became apparent to the excited crowd that the race would not be decided until the very last moment as Preakness and Springbok vied for the lead.

The crowd roared its approval as the horses reached the quarter pole. Preakness was still just a length ahead of Springbok, who now had two lengths on Aaron Pennington. Grinstead had moved into fourth ahead of the trailing Olitipa, Rutherford, and Wild Idle.

The jubilant crowd delightedly watched as Preakness retained the lead past the furlong pole, with Springbok closing rapidly. With the entire crowd rising and screaming approval, Springbok lurched for the wire. Preakness would not yield, and the horses hit the finish together. Following the two leaders, Grinstead closed for third place, two lengths back. Aaron Pennington finished fourth, followed by Olitipa, Rutherford, and Wild Idle.

Some in the crowd swore the aging campaigner Preakness had prevailed while others insisted the surging Springbok had pulled ahead at the last moment. Several anxious moments passed, and then the judges announced that the race was a dead heat, in the fastest time on record, 3:56 1/4. The winning time beat Harry Bassett's record by two and three-quarters seconds, and would not be surpassed until 1891 when Los Angeles won the Cup in 3:43 1/2.

When Preakness and Springbok returned to the grandstand, the two warriors were greeted with round after round of applause, and a loud and sustained clamor for a runoff. But calls for a runoff were dashed when McDaniel told Sanford that Springbok had come up lame. While the two owners agreed to split the $2,050 stakes between them, the crowd persisted in its hopes for a runoff, and it was at least fifteen minutes before the enthusiastic crowd finally allowed track management and staff to prepare the horses for the next race.

The dead-heat finish gave Springbok a claim to the cup for the second straight year, and gave his owner, McDaniel, the pleasure of winning the cup for four successive years. It was also a milestone day for Sanford and his co-champion Preakness. The Saratoga Cup was to be Preakness' last race in America. In the fall of 1875, Sanford sent several horses, including Preakness, to England to compete the following spring. Preakness raced four times in England, with a win, and second-, third- and fourth-place finishes. After Preakness won the Brighton Cup, Sanford offered the horse for sale, and he was purchased by the twelfth Duke of Hamilton.

Unfortunately for Preakness, Lord Hamilton was a hot-tempered man with a reputation for extravagance. Preakness had always been difficult to handle, so it was probably just a matter of time before the high-strung Lord Hamilton and his new horse would fall out. A clash of wills resulted in an altercation in Preakness' stall, the enraged Hamilton pulled out a gun, fired a shot at point-blank range, and killed his own horse.

The outcry against the Duke was so great that reform laws were passed regarding the governing, handling, and treatment of horses and other animals in England. But it was too late for Preakness, still remembered as the namesake of the second leg of the American Triple Crown.

Lost in the confusion and jubilation of a truly magnificent race, a few took no comfort, no solace, in the splendid performance of the marvelous athletes. For Aaron Pennington and his backers it had been a very disappointing day.

For Price McGrath it had to have been a particularly difficult day. No doubt his mind at that moment was flooded with many thoughts: his recent altercation with George Wilkes; the status of the resulting lawsuits; the bitter knowledge that the wishes of his accuser, George Wilkes, had prevailed on that day; the status of his Thoroughbred Aaron Pennington and his disappointing finish; the money he undoubtedly lost on the race; and, just as important, his future in horse racing.

McGrath, who had been so vocal before the race about his horse's prospects and so eager to justify his position in Thoroughbred racing with a triumph, now stood alone in the crowd and "looked decidedly uncomfortable."[xxvii]

With races such as the 1875 Saratoga Cup and patronage from men such as Belmont, Sanford, and even McGrath, the popularity of racing at Saratoga continued to grow, but the man who had envisioned Saratoga, John Morrissey, was slowly withdrawing from his creation. In the years after he brought his vision to Saratoga, the former gang member and wharf rat had run for political office, been elected to Congress, and served two terms. In 1875 he was elected to the New York state senate. Two years later he relinquished his position as president of the Saratoga Association to focus on his re-election campaign and was replaced by hotelier James Marvin.

Even though Morrissey won, the race for the senate seat had physically drained him, and afterward his health suffered.

Accustomed to overcoming long odds, the struggle to regain his health was one battle the longshot Morrissey could not win. The rough life John Morrissey had led and his habit of smoking as many as seventeen cigars daily for years had finally caught up to him. After struggling with his health for several months, Morrissey and his wife decided to seek the warmth of the South in hopes it would help him recover.

He seemed to rally slightly in February 1878, and the couple returned to New York the next month. Morrissey visited his childhood home in Troy, caught a severe cold, and then contracted pneumonia. On April 19 the Morrisseys took refuge at the Adelphi Hotel in Saratoga and hoped for a recovery, but Morrissey's health continued to decline. With his right arm paralyzed and his speech slurred from an apparent stroke, the former prizefighter valiantly muttered, "I am running neck and neck with death, and rapidly tiring."[xxviii] In his last days Morrissey repeated one of his favorite comments: "Yes, I am a gambler and a prize fighter; but no man can ever say that I turned a dishonest card or struck a low blow."[xxix]

On May 1, 1878, Father John McMenomy administered extreme unction (anointing of the sick) to Morrissey, who finally succumbed that day, his wife and several employees at his side. The Saratoga visionary was forty-seven.

It had been an extraordinary life by any account. In his lifetime Morrissey had accumulated more than a million dollars twice. Still, despite all his success, when his estate was settled it was valued at less than $75,000.

None of this mattered to the drenched crowd of more than 15,000 in Troy who came to honor him as his body was laid to rest in the rain. The former brawler and gambler was loved by the people and respected by politicians and members of the press.

The New York City newspapers, frequent critics in life, were for the most part gracious and kind in extensive eulogies. Some papers never forgave his rough-and-tumble background, but a column in the *New York Times* stated his death was "a loss to the cause of good government in New York" and "no man ever charged John Morrissey with being a venal legislator or a dishonest politician."[xxx] The *Times* then added, "No burial ever evoked so many expressions of sorrow from the mass of people-the hard, rough workingmen and women ... They turned out en masse today, in their working clothes and with the grit upon their faces, to watch with a tear in their eyes the passage of the funeral procession."[xxxi]

When the news of Morrissey's death reached New York, the gambling house at 5 West 24th Street suspended play. It was here Morrissey had gone into business with fellow professional gamblers Charles Reed and Albert Spencer years ago. As the games were halted in honor of a fallen comrade, Reed and Spencer were making their way to Saratoga to take over for their former partner.

CHAPTER 6

Duke of Magenta and Hindoo

Charles Reed and Albert Spencer were both professional gamblers, but the similarities ended there. Reed, from Tennessee, didn't drink and attended the Episcopal Church, but he was also an old-time Southern gambler who had killed a man in New Orleans during the Civil War. Reed had been sentenced to death by hanging but had been pardoned by the brother of Major General Benjamin Butler, who protected gamblers for payoffs, which he shared with the general.[i]

Reed moved to New York after the war and teamed with Spencer, a quiet and serious man who claimed to be an art critic and collector. They joined a syndicate organized by Morrissey to finance gambling at 5 West 24th Street.[ii]

When it came to horses, Reed was not just a gambler; he had a genuine appreciation for the animals and racing. He owned several horses and would purchase the prize stallion St. Blaise for $100,000 when August Belmont's death resulted in an auction of his stable in 1890.[iii]

After Morrissey's death, Spencer ran the betting pools and Morrissey's casino in Congress Park while Reed became the Saratoga track lessee.

The casino, however, floundered in the years following

Morrissey's death. In 1893 Spencer took in a Manhattan gambling operator as a partner. The next year Spencer sold the casino to Richard Canfield for $250,000, then left the country for France, never to return.

Unlike Morrissey, the suave and sophisticated Canfield was generally regarded as a friend and an equal by the rich and famous that frequented Saratoga. Like Morrissey, Canfield came from humble beginnings. He was born the fifth of six children to William Canfield, who at various times was a publisher, hotel proprietor, and restaurant owner in New Bedford, Massachusetts.

Richard Canfield graduated from Brimmer Grammar School in 1869 and then obtained a job in the shipping department at Jordan, Marsh, and Company in 1870, earning $2 a week. But Canfield quarreled with his boss and resigned.

At age fifteen, the young Canfield supported himself as a freelance gambler in Boston, Pawtucket, and Providence. Claiming he won $20,000 in 1876, Canfield traveled to Europe, spent his winnings, and returned penniless to America determined to become the proprietor of a fashionable gambling house.

He then supported himself with a series of jobs at upscale New England hotels while operating small poker games until April 26, 1884, when he was arrested, sentenced, and jailed for six months. At this point Canfield undertook an effort to improve himself by reading all the literature on history, religion, philosophy, and art that he could get his hands on — interests that he pursued for the rest of his life.

Canfield then went to New York City and opened a poker room with pawnbroker William Glover. Within a year Canfield's profits were $300 a week. He sold out to Glover and opened, with David Duff, the Madison Square Club at No. 23 West 26th Street that featured faro, poker, and roulette wheels. By 1892

Canfield was one of the best-regarded gamblers in the city and thought to be worth almost $1 million.

For several years Canfield had been visiting Saratoga and, like Spencer, realized that he shared a passion for art and gambling. Canfield persuaded Spencer to sell him an interest in the casino and then bought him out.

Canfield immediately added an element of luxury to the casino. He made extensive improvements to the dining room and employed a famous French chef along with fifty waiters from New York City. His renovated dining room was advertised as the most expensive and sumptuous in America, with prices that rivaled the most expensive New York City restaurants including Delmonico's. On a personal level, Canfield wore only custom-made suits and for evenings, tails and white tie.

Canfield's renovated casino was an immediate success. The casino featured two faro boxes and nine single-end hickory roulette wheels inlaid with ivory for ivory chips. Upstairs, private rooms featured a faro box and two double-end wheels. Play continued throughout the night, usually until dawn, as long as there were patrons. Customers could buy white chips worth $1, red chips for $5, blue chips for $10, yellow chips for $100, and large brown chips for $1,000. In the private rooms upstairs, the house and players set limits, and the value of the chips was increased by a factor of one hundred. To accommodate the needs of his customers, Canfield always kept $1 million in his safe.

While the renovated dining room never made money for Canfield — he once said he lost $70,000 per season on it — the gambling profits at the casino almost equaled the $250,000 he paid Spencer to acquire the place. During his tenure at the casino, Canfield cleared as much as $500,000 per season.

Of his success Canfield once said, "All any gambler wants is to have play for a long enough time and he'll get all the money

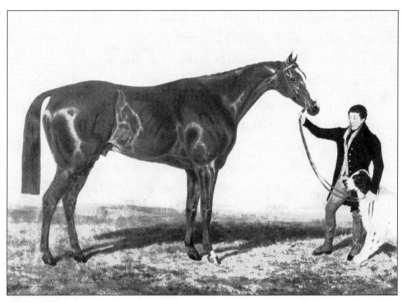

Duke of Magenta

any player has. In business, if you or I can lend money enough at five per cent, we think we are doing pretty well. Every time a roulette wheel is spun the percentage on a thirty-six-inch wheel is 5-5/19 per cent against the player. Therefore, you will say that I get an interest on my money of 5-5/19 per cent every time a roulette wheel is spun. If I have any patronage at all, you can imagine what interest I get on my money in any one night."[iv]

◆◆◆◆

Under Reed's management the track grew and prospered. Reed came to like Saratoga and eventually built a $50,000 home on Union Avenue with horse etchings in glass above the transoms.[v]

Like Morrissey, Reed also yearned to be accepted by Saratoga society and also was rebuffed. Unlike Morrissey, who was widely liked and admired but never accepted as a social equal, Reed became a target for moral crusaders. In 1887, tired of being spurned by Saratoga society and fending off anti-gambling forces, Reed sold his share of the track to Spencer, moved back to New York City, and resumed management of the 5 West 24th Street casino.

Spencer, who still managed the Congress Park casino — generally known as the Saratoga Club House — at the time, became the track's lessee, and he continued to oversee a growing and prosperous business, even serving as treasurer and secretary of the Saratoga Association. Under his management the Spencer Handicap was established, and $2,000 was added to its value. Later he insisted that the Saratoga Association keep the value of the race at $5,000 or more.[vi]

◆◆◆◆

During Reed's and Spencer's tenures, a major component in the track's success was the emergence of two strong-willed and talented colts: Duke of Magenta and Hindoo.

Duke of Magenta, or the "Duke" as he was referred to in the contemporary press, was first on the scene, having been foaled at R.A. Alexander's Woodburn Stud in Kentucky in 1875.[vii] He was in the final crop of the great sire Lexington and out of the Yorkshire mare Magenta. As a young horse, Duke of Magenta was acquired by the tobacco magnate George L. Lorillard.

The Duke was fortunate to race for a benevolent owner. The six-foot, two-hundred-pound George Lorillard was the younger brother of Pierre Lorillard and was known as a genial sportsman and a crack marksman.

Lorillard's horses, based at Westbrook Stable, in Islip, Long Island, included future Preakness winners Harold, Grenada, Saunterer, and Vanguard. To facilitate a successful stable, Lorillard shrewdly employed one of the best trainers of the time in R. Wyndham Walden.

Over the course of a career that spanned twenty-six years (1872 to 1898), Walden trained for J.A. and A.H. Morris, and later, Lorillard. Walden trained seven Preakness winners and a total of two hundred winners, including the Duke, Russell,

Reckon, St. Florian, Correction, The Friar, and Mars. In total, his horses earned $1,367,796.[viii]

It was into Walden's care that the high-spirited Duke of Magenta was entrusted. While his bloodlines were topnotch, the Duke was not considered the top two-year-old of 1877. That honor was given to Pierre Lorillard's Leamington filly, Perfection. The two horses first met in Jerome Park's four-furlong Juvenile Stakes in June. It was a close race, but the judges gave Perfection the win and the Duke second place.

Six weeks later the two had a rematch at Saratoga in the four-furlong Flash Stakes. This time the Duke managed to hold on by a neck over Perfection.

On July 31, 1877, just one week after his victory in the Flash Stakes, the Duke faced Perfection again, in the fourteenth renewal of the six-furlong Saratoga Stakes. Pierre Lorillard's pair of Perfection and Pique was a strong co-favorite, with the Duke second choice in the betting pools.

The Duke was a notoriously high-strung and bad-tempered horse who acted up that day "in a most outrageous fashion."[ix] As the waiting time dragged on, the anxious Duke reared as his jockey desperately tried to hang on. Then the colt tried to jump the rails separating the chute from the main track but failed to clear them. Instead, he landed on the rails, collapsing them under his weight; another starter, Bramble, followed the Duke but easily cleared the fallen rails.

There were two more attempts at a start before the horses were finally ready. On the third and successful attempt the horses broke away in a staggered procession. Bramble, who had not received much attention in the betting, had the cleanest start and jumped out to a four-length lead, followed by Pride of the Village, the Duke, Perfection, and the rest of the nine-horse field. Bramble maintained a lead of two lengths coming out of the chute on to the track at the half-mile pole as the Duke made up some ground on Bramble. Perfection was two more lengths back.

As they came around the lower turn, Bramble opened up by three lengths as Perfection closed on the Duke. In the homestretch the Duke again made a run at Bramble and pulled up to Bramble's saddle girth, followed closely by Perfection and Pride of the Village. The four had now pulled away from the pack and created a "whipping race home between them."[x]

The group was so closely bunched as it passed the press stand it was impossible to discern a leader, and the large crowd bolted to the grandstand from the large open-air bleacher section to watch the finish. The horses passed the finish line still so closely bunched that the winner was not apparent. The judges deliberated, and Bramble was declared the winner, with the Duke second, followed by Pride of the Village and Perfection.

As racing fans savored the magnificent race they had just witnessed, the gamblers sought consolation from their losses. The *New York Times* reporter wrote, "This was the greatest slaughter that the knowing ones have had this season, and one that it will take them some time to recover from."[xi]

Shortly after the race Bramble's jubilant owners proudly declared that Bramble "wasn't for sale at any price."[xii] But before the season had ended, gambling debts forced them to do otherwise, and Bramble, a son of Bonnie Scotland, was sold to the Dwyer brothers, Mike and Phil. With Bramble the brothers had a winner who would go on to a successful racing career in his own right and rival the Duke for several seasons.

Less than two weeks later, fourteen juveniles, including Duke of Magenta, Bramble, Perfection and her stablemate Spartan, and Pride of the Village, met in the six-furlong Kentucky Stakes at Saratoga. So far the Duke had not finished out of the money, yet he still was not considered the favorite in the pre-race pools. After the bath the gamblers and speculators had taken in the

Mike Dwyer

Saratoga Stakes, they were more cautious approaching this race and made no heavy favorites. Pierre Lorillard's pair, Perfection and the unknown and untested Spartan, drew the most support in the pools, with the Duke again second choice.

The race began with a straggling start, and as the field ran down the chute toward the main track, Fawn took the lead with Pride of the Village second and Perfection third. Before they reached the end of the chute, Perfection had rushed to the front. As the horses reached the regular track at the half-mile pole, a cloud of dust shrouded the field.

Perfection emerged from the cloud with a four-length lead, a position she held down the backstretch as the field sorted itself out behind her.

Turning into the homestretch, Perfection appeared to falter. Bramble moved into second as Perfection fell back. Pride of the Village challenged Bramble for the lead, with the Duke closing on the outside. But Pride of the Village went on to win the race by three lengths in 1:18 1/4. The Duke got up for second by a neck over Bramble. Perfection ended up fifth.

Four days after his loss to Pride of the Village, the Duke started again in the second running of the six-furlong Grinstead Stakes at Saratoga. Four other horses joined the Duke at the post: James A. Grinstead's colt by Alarm, F. Smythe's Wade Hampton, and Pierre Lorillard's entries, Spartan and Bertha.

Gamblers and speculators had become painfully aware that

they would bet against the Duke at their own peril as he was consistently placing in races. Coming into the Grinstead, he was heavily favored.

As the horses gathered in the chute for the start, the high-strung Duke again acted up and delayed the start. After several false starts the race finally began, and Grinstead's colt took the lead. Bertha was second, followed by the Duke, Wade Hampton, and Spartan.

This time the Duke kept closer to the lead running down the chute. Grinstead's colt had set a very fast pace, and around the far turn he maintained a short lead over the Duke. Spartan now made his move and passed Bertha into third, but it was still a very tight race and "there was a length and a half of daylight between all of them until they turned into the home stretch."[xiii]

With Spartan at his tail, the Duke closed on the Grinstead colt and passed him at the furlong pole. As Spartan's jockey watched the Duke pull away, he whipped his mount, and they almost reached even terms. At the finish the Duke appeared to win by a neck, but the judges called the race a dead heat in a "very fast"[xiv]

Phil Dwyer (second from left)

1:16 3/4. Grinstead's colt finished third, two lengths behind the leaders, followed by Bertha and Wade Hampton.

George Lorillard was ill and not on the course that day, so it was decided by his representative and his brother Pierre to divide the stakes and with it the money from the pools. The result was that those who had tickets in the mutuel pools on the Duke lost money despite the first-place finish. For those who had tickets on Spartan, the dead heat resulted in their value climbing to $12.

Only at the end of his juvenile season did the Duke establish the form that would propel him to a dominating three-year-old year. At Jerome Park on September 29, 1877, the Duke prevailed over a strong field of nine including Pride of the Village and Spartan, who finished in a dead heat for second, a half-length behind. Just a week later, at Pimlico's fall meet, the Duke won the one-mile Central Stakes and finished the year with four wins in seven starts and earnings of $9,987.

Even before the 1878 season began, most track observers had expected a very successful three-year-old campaign for the Duke. A *New York Times* reporter noted that the three-year-old Duke of Magenta had filled out substantially since his previous race in October and had to be considered the leading contender for the upcoming season's races. Duke of Magenta proved the pundits right, and other than an early season defeat due to an infection, he went about dominating his races at distances between one and two miles, in good and bad weather.

By mid-summer he was back at Saratoga, awaiting the one and three-quarters-mile Travers Stakes on July 20. Only four other horses showed: the Dwyer brothers' Bramble, Pierre Lorillard's Spartan, Thomas Puryear and Company's Danicheff, and George Lorillard's Albert.

The morning of the race the Duke suffered a bout of colic. Rumors swirled trackside just before the race that the Duke would start but was too ill to run well. As the rumors spread, the gamblers made their own race to hedge their bets with Danicheff and the Duke and his stablemate Albert, now the co-favorites.

The race endured several delays. Spartan became so excited that it took ten minutes for his jockey just to mount him. Then after several false starts, a clean start was finally made in the chute. Bramble took the lead but lost it quickly to Spartan.

Turning onto the regular track at the half-mile pole, Spartan increased his lead to three lengths, followed by Danicheff, a length ahead of Bramble, with the Duke and Albert trailing. After three-quarters of a mile, Spartan clung to his lead, but Danicheff, Bramble, and the Duke were nearly even with each other and were closing on him. As they hit the turn, Bramble made his move and attempted to pass Spartan. Spartan held him off, however, and spurted away again.

Bramble was still two lengths ahead of the Duke when the latter colt began to move. The Duke passed Bramble and took aim at Spartan. At the quarter pole Spartan held a two-length lead over the Duke, who continued to gain on his rival. As Spartan tired, the Duke finally passed him mid-stretch and pulled away to win by two. Bramble also had passed Spartan late to get second, finishing three lengths ahead of the latter horse. The winning time was 3:08, the best time at that point for a three-year-old carrying 118 pounds.[xv]

About three weeks later, on August 13, 1878, the three-year-olds gathered for the two-mile Kenner Stakes at Saratoga. Only Bramble, Spartan, and Duke of Magenta went postward.

On race day, the Duke was favored at 2-1, with $4,000 offered in prize money for the winner. Bramble took the early lead, but at the first turn Spartan jumped ahead, with the Duke a length behind. When they reached the backstretch, the Duke closed on Spartan, with Bramble staying close.

At the half-mile pole the Duke responded to his jockey and passed Spartan. Bramble then pulled even with Spartan, a half-length back. Coming out of the far turn, Bramble reached the Duke's saddle girth, but the Duke rebuffed Bramble's charge and pulled away, opening up a length and a half lead.

The Duke passed the judges' stand with a mile in 1:50 3/4, two lengths ahead of Bramble, who was three lengths ahead of Spartan. Heading into the second mile, the Duke led by four lengths, but down the backstretch Spartan and Bramble closed the gap.

At the half-mile pole Bramble had moved to the Duke's tail while Spartan was only a length and a half back. Going into the far turn, Spartan pulled even with Bramble, then passed him. As the horses rounded the turn, the fans became so swept away with excitement that they jumped to their feet and cheered wildly, expecting a frantic finish.

In the homestretch Bramble took aim on the Duke. When Bramble pulled to the Duke's flank, the crowd buzzed with excitement as they sensed the race would not be decided until the finish line.

But then the Duke showed why he had become a dominant horse and a true champion when he pulled away again, winning by two lengths, as Bramble edged Spartan for second. The final time was 3:41 1/2 for two miles. Afterward, the excited *New York Times* reporter proclaimed in his column, "The race was the greatest feature of the season."[xvi]

One week later, on August 20, 1878, the Duke ran in the one and a half-mile Harding Stakes for three-year-olds. Not one single pool was sold on the race because the Duke was such a great favorite. He had become so dominant that no one really expected any of other thirty-two horses nominated to show up.

At post time, however, D. McCarthy decided to start his chestnut colt Helmsman, who carried five pounds less than the Duke, who was carrying 118 pounds. After the flag fell, the confident Duke of Magenta went to the front, was never headed, and won by four lengths in a gallop in a time of 2:50 3/4.

He was to race four more times that September and won them all, including the two-mile Breckinridge in which he carried a five-pound penalty. In this race his trainer, Wyndham Walden, decided to let the big colt run, and the Duke cantered to an easy win, twelve lengths in front.

George Lorillard then resolved to test his horses against the best that English racing could offer. Lorillard shipped some of his top horses, including the Duke, to England. While crossing, however, the Duke contracted influenza and became very ill. He was not killed by the contagion, but his racing career was over. When he returned to America, he returned only for a stud career.

The Duke finished with fifteen wins, three seconds, and one third from nineteen starts and won a total of $45,412[xvii] during his racing career. During his dominant three-year-old campaign, the Duke won the Withers, Preakness, Belmont, and Travers stakes. While eleven horses have won the Triple Crown, only two others — Man o' War and Native Dancer — have managed to win these four races during the same season.

In the spring of 1878 as Duke of Magenta was beginning his dominating sophomore season, a leggy young colt with a star and one white hind leg was foaled. Sired by Virgil (by Vandal) and out of Florence, by Lexington, Hindoo was bred in Kentucky by Daniel Swigert, who later would acquire Milton Sanford's Preakness Stud, home of Virgil, and rename it Elmendorf Farm. At first appearance Hindoo seemed much too delicate to become one of the most noted horses of his day and a star at Saratoga. But the leggy young foal would grow to just under 16 hands and weigh nine hundred pounds in training. The colt was an anomaly; he possessed an indomitable will but was also good-natured. *Spirit of the Times* described him as, "A sweeter-tempered colt never sported silk. He was like wax in the hands of the jockey. He would never do more than was asked of him, yet his courage was the highest."[xviii]

At the age of two, Hindoo made his first track appearance a winning one, at Lexington, Kentucky, on May, 13, 1880, and went on to win seven consecutive races in the Midwest (then considered the "West"), including the Colt and Filly Stakes in Lexington and the Alexander Stakes and Tennessee Stakes in Louisville.

Hindoo's victories ranged over distances of four and six furlongs up to a mile. It was widely accepted that his undefeated string would result in the remarkable colt being named the informal champion two-year-old for the season. After a short rest Hindoo returned to the track.

Hindoo arrived in Saratoga on August 4 to begin training for the five-furlong Windsor Hotel Stakes ten days later, and he attracted a great deal of public interest. Knowing that he had just returned from a brief layoff, many wondered about his fitness. Still, fitness concerns aside, he was made the prohibitive favorite.

A torrential rain the morning of the race had left the track muddy, but when the bell summoned the horses and their jockeys to face the starter, eight horses showed up, including Hindoo; Thora, a bay filly by Longfellow; the bay filly Bonnie Lizzie; the brown gelding Crickmore; and the bay colt Calycanthus. Not only was the race Hindoo's debut at Saratoga, but it also was his first race in the East. While he was the favorite, his lack of preparation and his impost of 107 pounds made him seem vulnerable to an upset.

Crickmore and Bonnie Lizzie were considered his toughest opponents. Crickmore, who would go on to win the 1881

Hindoo

Withers and Dixie stakes, had also been training at Saratoga and appeared to be in excellent condition. The previous week he had run three-quarters of a mile in 1:19 in a trial against the mare Oriole.

Bonnie Lizzie, sired by Hurrah and out of Bonnie Kate, was also a realistic threat to Hindoo. She would go on to finish third in the six-furlong Champagne Stakes that year and in 1881 would finish second in the nine-furlong Alabama Stakes.[xix]

When Hindoo appeared on the track, he was greeted with a hearty round of applause, but Crickmore also had his backers, and betting was heavy before the race.

The starter had trouble preparing the horses, causing a long delay. When the flag finally fell, the filly Bonnie Lizzie, like Hindoo carrying 107 pounds, took the lead. Heading into the far turn, Hindoo moved even with Bonnie Lizzie, four lengths ahead of Calycanthus, who was a length in front of Little Nell, with Crickmore and Bridecake trailing. The race now appeared to be between Hindoo and Bonnie Lizzie.

Jimmy McLaughlin

In the homestretch, as they approached the furlong pole, Hindoo began to falter. Allen, his jockey, realizing that Hindoo was losing ground, used the whip, while Bonnie Lizzie continued to set the pace and was cheered by the crowd at the betting stand.

Crickmore now rushed up on the outside as his backers screamed with delight. He passed Hindoo, closed on Bonnie Lizzie, then passed her to win by a head in 1:05. The excitement that had been building as the horses rushed to the finish erupted. Men jubilantly danced around and threw their hats in the air while the ladies joined in the cheers. Bonnie Lizzie finished a length in front of Hindoo, who just managed to beat the filly Thora by a nose. With the victory, Crickmore would share the unofficial two-year-old championship with Hindoo.[xx]

Following his two-year-old campaign, Hindoo was purchased for $15,000 by brothers Mike and Phil Dwyer. The Dwyer brothers had inherited a thriving butcher shop in Brooklyn and a natural ability to judge quality horses. Brother Phil bought the horses and Mike bet on them. They began their racing career with trotters before they switched to Thoroughbreds and started a racing stable.

Realizing they had a potential champion on their hands in Hindoo, the Dwyer brothers brought in one of the best jockeys of the time for the colt's three-year-old campaign. Jimmy McLaughlin was easy to spot with his trademark handlebar mustache, but his real claim to fame was four Travers Stakes victories, a record not matched for more than sixty years.

With McLaughlin as his jockey, Hindoo was almost unbeatable, and his three-year-old season began with a remarkable string of eighteen consecutive victories in less than four months. It is a feat that is unmatched by any modern horse; only Cigar and Citation have come close with sixteen consecutive wins.

Hindoo's victories in 1881 included the Blue Ribbon Stakes, the Kentucky Derby, the Clark Stakes, the Coney Island Derby, and the Lorillard Stakes. At Saratoga, Hindoo was victorious in the Travers Stakes and also in the Sequel Stakes, the United States Hotel Stakes, and the two-mile Kenner Stakes for three-year-olds, in which Hindoo ran one of his best races.

Thirty-seven horses had been nominated for the Kenner Stakes, but Hindoo had been so dominant that season that on August 11 only two horses showed up to challenge him: G.W. Darden's brown colt Bonfire, a son of Bonnie Scotland out of Fannie Barrow, carrying 118 pounds, and Hindoo's old friend and nemesis Crickmore, who was carrying 115 pounds.

It had been almost a year since Crickmore had defeated Hindoo in the Windsor Hotel Stakes, and the two would face each other on several occasions that season, with mixed results. But on this day, Hindoo who was carrying 118 pounds, would not be denied. In describing the race the *New York Times* called the race more of "… a walkover or mere exhibition."[xxi] When Hindoo appeared on the track, looking every bit the champion he was, the crowd responded with round after round of applause.

There were no delays and the starter had the horses off on the first attempt. Hindoo promptly took the lead by a half-length, followed by Crickmore, a half-length ahead of Bonfire. McLaughlin continued to let Hindoo set the pace, while Hughes on Crickmore held his horse back tightly, still followed by Bonfire.

For a brief moment it appeared that Crickmore might make

a race of it. Hindoo was ahead by four lengths, and when they had run a mile and a quarter, Hughes had Crickmore pull within two lengths of Hindoo. Crickmore continued to trail Hindoo for another quarter of a mile, and as they reached the homestretch, Hughes flogged his horse repeatedly in an attempt to stay close.

But there was no catching Hindoo that day. With a furlong to go, Hughes finally realized that Crickmore could not catch Hindoo and eased up. Hindoo won the two-mile race by five lengths in 3:32.

Hindoo's fractions for the race were remarkable: the quarter in :28 3/4; the half, :55; three-quarters, 1:21 1/2; a mile and a quarter, 2:18; a mile and a half, 2:38; and a mile and three-quarters, 3:04.

His time of 3:32 beat the old record for the Kenner Stakes by a full three seconds, and there seemed to be no doubt among the spectators that had he been pressed at all by the competition, Hindoo could easily have challenged and beaten the two-mile American record.

For the year Hindoo would finish with earnings of $49,100. Hindoo, who raced at four, never finished out of the money, and his career record was thirty wins, three seconds, and two thirds in thirty-five starts with earnings of $72,340.[xxii]

CHAPTER 7

The Walbaum Era

In 1889, two years after Albert Spencer had assumed control of the Saratoga track, a moral crusader targeted Spencer's management. Spencer Trask, of the Wall Street brokerage firm Spencer Trask and Company, maintained an office on the ground floor of the Grand Union[i] and had purchased an estate close to the track.

Using his significant political and financial influence, Trask intended to remake Saratoga into a "sedate, year-round community for the wealthy, along the lines of Newport,"[ii] the Rhode Island enclave the wealthy used as a seaside playground. He then hired, at a personal cost of as much as $50,000, several New York City detectives to gather evidence against Albert Spencer and his operation of open illegal gambling.[iii] In 1890 Spencer buckled under Trask's pressure. The track at Saratoga was put up for sale for $375,000. When no potential buyers emerged, rumors began to circulate that Pierre Lorillard, August Belmont, and others wanted to form a syndicate to keep racing in Saratoga.[iv]

As Spencer sought a buyer for the track, several longtime members of the Saratoga Association resigned. James Marvin, the association's second president and a friend to Morrissey,

Spencer Trask and family

resigned at the age of eighty-two. Charles Wheatly, who had designed the track and later served as secretary of the association, also stepped down.[v]

The sale of the track, accompanied by the management exodus, created a leadership void. Into this void stepped Gottfried "Dutch Fred" Walbaum, who in 1891 bought the track for the asking price.[vi] Walbaum's purchase raised many eyebrows in Saratoga, including Spencer Trask's, when it was learned the new owner also co-owned the Guttenberg Race Track in northern New Jersey.

A cloud of intrigue circulated around Walbaum, who once operated a gambling house in the Bowery. Saratoga historian Hugh Bradley writes that some of Walbaum's detractors believed Guttenberg was the first American course "on which owners experimented with electric batteries and narcotics while seeking to have their horses win races at good prices."[vii] Bradley also writes that Walbaum may have "made his first important money by running a brothel."[viii]

However he had initially made his money, Walbaum leased the Guttenberg track in 1887, close to the old Beacon racetrack that once had flourished in Hoboken, New Jersey.[ix] As the new co-owner, Walbaum promised to be on his best behavior and vowed the track would be run "with no trickery."[x]

Walbaum and his co-owners proved effective administrators, and under their management the Guttenberg track started turning a profit. These profits put Walbaum in a position to buy the track at Saratoga. The *New York Times* reported in March 1891 that the Guttenberg track had been a "gold mine"[xi] to Walbaum and his associates with profits of at least $5,000 a day.

While Walbaum and company were skilled at turning a profit, they were much less adept at avoiding scandal. In 1877 the New York state legislature had outlawed gambling pools. Like Morrissey, Walbaum decided that the laws against pool selling didn't necessarily apply to him, and he apparently continued the practice.

In 1891, the year Walbaum bought the Saratoga track, he was indicted in New Jersey for activities at Guttenberg. That May the *New York Times* reported, "The Hudson County Grand Jury, in their batch of indictments handed to Judge Knapp on Thursday night, included one against Gottfried Walbaum, President of the Hudson County Jockey Club, for keeping a 'disorderly house' at the Guttenberg race track, and against James Brown and Edward Shapley for selling pools at the tracks."[xii]

Walbaum also made enemies in Saratoga because he introduced innovations that suited his purposes. When he moved the starting time of the racing program from 11:30 a.m. to 2:30 p.m., the hotels and visitors who centered their activities on an earlier starting time were outraged. The *New York Times* correspondent reported on the resulting uproar from town and fans and wrote that the local community and visitors "... will

Winter racing at Walbaum's Guttenberg track

not give up their whole day to gratify the wishes of the track owners, who are for no good reason conceivably trying to force people to accept the change. The managers have thus far cared only for the wishes of the professional gamblers, who infest the town, and the change was made to suit them alone. The falling off in attendance of the hotel people is so marked, however, that the change to morning racing will almost surely come, or the hotel guests will stay away entirely."[xiii]

Even other bookmakers protested the change because their best customers, "your water drinker,"[xiv] or those who abstained from alcohol, found the change troublesome. Walbaum casually disregarded the complaints. He was known to gamble regularly at the clubhouse until 4 a.m., sleep until noon, and was disinclined to change his routine. When confronted with the bookmakers' complaints about their customers, Walbaum replied, "Oh to ... with the ... water drinkers. I don't want them out to the track anyhow."[xv]

Walbaum had implemented another innovation at his

Guttenberg track when he initiated a winter racing program. This proved extremely popular in the poolrooms of New York and with the crowds at the track, but much less popular with the professionals who worked at the tracks. The jockeys were even forced to wear gloves and mufflers to ward off the cold.[xvi]

The most notorious of Walbaum's innovations at Saratoga was probably his introduction of gambling for women and children. Walbaum provided wood-trimmed "retiring rooms" in the grandstand that were actually betting rooms unique in the country. In these rooms, bookmakers, ticket sellers, and cashiers posted behind a wire screen and a large counter took bets from women and groups of children as young as ten. The odds and entry information were posted on large blackboards and updated by operators who relayed information from the main ring. Even here the customers didn't get a break because the women and children regularly received worse odds.

Walbaum's innovations were even less popular with racing's traditionalists. When the Board of Control outlawed winter racing several years after its inception, Walbaum and his Guttenberg partners just ignored the ruling and continued to profit from the program.[xvii] The sporting press railed against the continued pool selling and finally forced the district attorney's hand. In January 1892 the Chicago *Daily Tribune* reported Walbaum had been arrested at Guttenberg.[xviii]

Many of Walbaum's problems could be traced to his unwillingness to adhere to the rules established by the Board of Control and, later, The Jockey Club. Pierre Lorillard had organized the Board of Control in 1891 to establish order in racing. It comprised some major track owners and racing stable owners. Their intention was to oversee racing, but the board's authority was restricted for the most part to tracks in the New York City area.[xix] It was succeeded by The Jockey Club, which James R. Keene organized in 1894.[xx]

When Walbaum decided to thumb his nose at the Board of Control, and then at The Jockey Club, he became a target of, and a lightning rod for, controversy. It is a certainty that his abrasive personality also figured in the hostility he encountered. He was not born into wealth, lacked genteel manners, became successful only through his own efforts, was unconcerned with popular opinion, and was described as the "sweating, swearing Gottfried Walbaum."[xxi]

When racing's old guard learned that the unnamed buyer of the track at Saratoga was actually Walbaum, Turf historian Hotaling writes the reaction was quick and often hysterical.[xxii] Hotaling writes that the *Sporting World* reported that the self-appointed defenders of racing at Saratoga feared "their peace and perhaps their very lives would be in danger as soon as the horde of outlawed officials and horsemen were prepared for their attack on the village."[xxiii]

Despite Walbaum's knack for creating enemies, the attacks proved unsuccessful. While Walbaum had his share of critics, some racing veterans defended him. Sam Hildreth, at the time a young trainer who raced his own stable at Guttenberg, said Walbaum's operation was "on the level"[xxiv] and insinuated that competing gambling houses outside the grounds had damaged the track's reputation with unfounded accusations.[xxv]

Despite the controversy, by late 1891 Walbaum had gained a firm hold at Saratoga. He replaced the departing Wheatly with his own man, Samuel Whitehead, as secretary of the association. The following year Walbaum became president of the Saratoga Association and assumed complete control while "operating it in such a way as to pour fuel on the fires of antagonism."[xxvi]

Although Walbaum's first season in control was a big hit, it may have further antagonized the growing list of his enemies. Huge crowds attended the races, a fact reported by his backers in the sporting press. They also reported there were ninety winning owners that season, some of whom were considered "outlaws,"[xxvii] those owners and track management who had refused to accept the Board of Control's rules and regulations for the governance of racetracks.

While Walbaum was consistently able to turn a profit, the track's programs suffered under his management and the great races diminished. As a result of the open hostility to Walbaum's management, many prominent stables avoided Saratoga and vowed not to return until new management was in place. Therefore, many of the traditional and popular races suffered from the lack of championship-quality racehorses and support from the owners:

• The Saratoga Cup was suspended from 1887 to 1890, revived in 1891, and then disappeared again during Walbaum's tenure.

• The one-and-a-quarter-mile Alabama Stakes for three-year-old fillies — named in honor of William Cottrell of Mobile, Alabama, who was too modest to have a race named for him personally — was not run from 1893 to 1896 or from 1898 to 1900. Early winners included Thora, sired by the great champion Longfellow.[xxviii]

• The seven-furlong Spinaway Stakes, already a respected test of juvenile fillies, was not run from 1892 to 1900.[xxix]

• The Travers' value dropped to a low of $1,125 in 1895 when the filly Liza won.[xxx]

To worsen matters, Walbaum also became involved in bookmaking at his own track. At one point he backed ten bookies who did an average business of $4,000 daily.[xxxi] But most of his money came from some 320 East Coast poolrooms that paid him ten dollars daily for wired overnight entries for the daily results.[xxxii]

As if to spite his many loud critics, Walbaum often boasted of his exploits. On the days his bookmaking was particularly lucrative, he was known to proclaim gleefully, "Look at me, I'm a sucker for luck, I am. I gave those boys out there the best of it, price and everything, but I won. Yessir, nobody can beat me. I'm just a sucker for luck."[xxxiii]

Walbaum may have crowed about his good luck, but he appears to have understood that luck wasn't always enough to win. Despite his oath to avoid "trickery," there was continuing speculation that Walbaum was more than willing to manage the outcome of races in which he bet on his own horses. Turf historian Hotaling wrote that Walbaum's horses only won when he had money riding on them,[xxxiv] and Walbaum appeared not to care at all if he wasn't particularly subtle in his maneuvers to win his bets at the track.

The 1894 meeting may have been the low point in Walbaum's tenure. Even before the season began, a shadow grew over the state of racing that extended to Saratoga when in January 1894 a court ruled the Trenton legislature's bill to permit the licensing of racetracks in New Jersey was unconstitutional.

Justice Lippincott's decision threatened the racing season at Monmouth in July and August, leaving Saratoga as the only meeting in the East for that time of year. A group of influential politicians and owners, including James R. Keene, August Belmont, and Richard Croker quickly gathered to discuss their options. Walbaum also had been invited but was unable to attend as he was in California. Instead he sent track secretary Samuel Whitehead to the meeting.[xxxv]

It's possible that Walbaum had made plans for travel to California, but it's also possible that Walbaum had decided to make himself scarce. In that same edition of the Chicago *Daily Tribune*, a report indicated that a Hudson County, New Jersey, grand jury had indicted Walbaum for "defiant violation of the law in connection with the Guttenberg race-track."[xxxvi]

The report stated, "The wheels of justice have been clogged

Patrons at the Saratoga entrance, circa early 1900s

for a long time in Hudson County, but they are running smoothly and rapidly now. The indictments are the result of the war opened on Guttenberg more than two years ago."[xxxvii] The newspaper also reported, "The indictments against the Jersey City Police Superintendent and Captains are for allowing policemen to serve as specials at the track."[xxxviii]

That same day another article in the Chicago *Daily Tribune* recorded a conversation between one of its reporters and Walbaum, who was in San Francisco. The reporter asked about the Eastern Turfmen and their request to extend the season at Saratoga while adhering to the guidelines of the Board of Control.

Walbaum, who had openly expressed contempt for the Board of Control, responded, "I am not going to do the Board of Control's bidding. It pinched me once and will again when it gets the chance."[xxxix]

Walbaum then said he was perfectly willing to extend the season by as many as fifteen new stakes. But Walbaum also made it clear that the rules governing the new races "shall be just as liberal"[xl] as any of the other races he organized at the 1894 meeting.

The struggle for control of the rules governing racing, including the track at Saratoga, continued several months later when The Jockey Club was organized. The report of the meeting in the Chicago *Daily Tribune* described the impact of The Jockey Club's rulings: "The entire West is ringing with the Jockey Club's new mandate which declared that all who do not race under its wing shall not race at all on the tracks it controls."[xli]

The Jockey Club specifically cited the Saratoga Racing Association and Walbaum's operation, when it declared, "Should either the Saratoga Racing Association or the Brighton Beach Association refuse to race under the rules of the Jockey club, and, therefore, of necessity, to enforce the forfeit list of the Jockey club, every person racing at those tracks and every official acting at those tracks becomes ipso facto an outlaw from the recognized meetings."[xlii]

Walbaum continued to disregard the threats of The Jockey Club. On July 25, just days after the meeting opened, he seems to have decided he would again be a sucker for luck and backed his horses heavily. The first race featured Walbaum's five-year-old Lamplighter, a son of Spendthrift out of Torchlight, in a one-and-a-quarter-mile race for all ages and a purse of $500.[xliii]

Lamplighter was said to be on the downside of his career. He was a good runner in his prime, but those days allegedly had come and gone. Yet here he was in Saratoga preparing for a big race and running very well. The bookmakers even had him pegged as a 2-5 favorite in the field of three, including Gideon & Daly's Cactus and G.B. Morris & Company's Illume. As it turned out, Lamplighter came through and won the race easily.

In the second race, a five-furlong scramble for two-year-olds, Walbaum's chestnut colt Picaroon (by Spendthrift out of Picadilly) was the even-money favorite. But there also was money on Colonel Pepper's fine filly, The Queen. Nothing seemed amiss when the jockey, A. Clayton, weighed out to ride The Queen before the race, and bets were recorded on her.

At post time, however, The Queen was nowhere to be found, and after a "long wait"[xliv] a messenger was sent to the stable. There, the messenger was told "the stable people had ordered the mare scratched early in the morning."[xlv] This forced the flummoxed stewards to fine Clayton $100 for the nonappearance. Colonel Pepper's trainer, A.W. Franklin, was asked about The Queen's failure to show, and he stated that he thought the mare had been scratched.[xlvi]

But after the race there was no official record of The Queen having been scratched, and the report in the Chicago *Daily Tribune* referred to the disappearance as an "ugly incident."[xlvii] Nor was there any indication she was seriously hurt. Less than a month later The Queen would be entered in another race at Saratoga.

Despite The Queen's no-show, as the horses were being readied for the race, track management claimed to be following Jockey Club rules when it decided that all bets made on The Queen were to stand, and the race proceeded.

The race featured nine maiden two-year-olds, including two other quality runners, Franklin and Miss Dixon, and a 100-1 longshot, the filly Blossom. As the horses broke from the starting line, the bookmakers, gamblers, and spectators all watched in stunned silence as the longshot, Blossom, immediately jumped out and opened up a lead of almost four lengths. Her lead almost appeared insurmountable, but Franklin and Picaroon managed to cut away slowly at Blossom's lead in the stretch. In a furious drive to the finish, Walbaum's Picaroon managed to edge the longshot by a neck at the wire.

The third race, a seven-furlong event, featured another

The Saratoga grandstand in the early 1900s

Walbaum favorite, May Win (by Richmond out of Mayfield). The seven-year-old May Win faced only two competitors. May Win took the early lead, set the pace, and easily crossed the finish line first, in another win for Walbaum.

At that point it was apparent to all but the most dim that the track owner's horses had swept the first three races, a trend that smart money should follow. Most money quickly switched to the lucky owner's stable, and the fourth race on the card that day featured a group of excellent sprinters including Rubicon, Kentigerna, Prig, and the 8-5 favorite, Walbaum's Potentate, who finished first and kept the winning string alive, to no one's surprise.

The correspondent from the *New York Times* wrote in his race report: "The feature of the day's sport was the fact that horses owned by Mr. Walbaum, President of the racing association, won all four of the events in which he had entries. He had no entries in the last two races, which was probably the only thing that kept him from sweeping the entire card."[xlviii]

Several days later the weather was mild, and the racing card promised excellent sport. But the attendance was smaller than expected as a result of the controversial change in the starting time for the races.

Despite the smaller crowds and the simmering resentment toward Walbaum's managerial techniques, his "lucky" run continued with a string of unexplained, if not questionable, incidents that further raised questions about the trustworthiness of the results. On July 31 his horses again dominated the racing, beginning with Potentate, a 2-5 favorite, who won the opening six-furlong race. Next, Lamplighter, the "hot favorite,"[xlix] won the mile-and-three-sixteenths Canadian Stakes.

In the upset of the day, Walbaum's two-year-old colt Rosemore beat Pierre Lorillard's heavy favorite, Redowac, when that Lorillard colt stopped suddenly in the homestretch.

The *New York Times* reported: "Lambley's riding on Redowac was so suspicious that he will be asked to explain it to the officials in the morning."[l]

One official, Judge Burke, promised to make a thorough investigation but then later stated he didn't believe Lambley's riding was extraordinary in any way. And Redowac's trainer, Mr. Huggins, told Judge Burke that the horse had sore shins, which might have accounted for Redowac coming to a halt in the stretch.

But one observer and track insider, Ralph Black, the owner of the jumping horse Southerner, angrily confronted another track official after the race about the suspicious events that had just unfolded on the track. The next day the *New York Times* reported "Black ... had some hot words for ex-Mayor Nolan of Troy, who acts as one of the stewards at the meeting, in which he used very improper language. The matter is referred to Louis Strauss and W.O.H. MacDonough, the association stewards, who today ordered Black to pay a fine of $200 for his discourteous language."[li]

The track crowd watched with dismay as Walbaum appeared to manage the outcome of races in which he bet on his horses, and the local townspeople and visitors continued to press their complaints on the race time change. Responding to the complaints and pressure from the local townspeople, Walbaum wearily indicated he had made a final decision on the issue and that racing would continue in the afternoon. It was strictly a business decision, he explained, as a change back to morning hours would cost the association at least $200 daily in receipts from poolrooms across the country.

The *New York Times* reported that Walbaum believed "Saratoga people should accommodate themselves to his hours willingly. As to the complaints of the villagers, he says, frankly, that he cares nothing about them, as they have never helped the track and do not add a couple of hundred dollars to its income during the racing season; therefore he sees no reason why he should put himself out that they may further benefit from the presence of summer visitors."[lii]

On August 8, Walbaum found himself enmeshed in another and just as damaging controversy when he asked Riley Grannon not to make book at the track. Grannon, who once ran a gambling house in Rawhide, Nevada, was described by the *New York Times* as "the heaviest bettor at the track, as well as the nerviest bookmaker" who was known to bet "thousands of dollars when others bet hundreds, and he will take almost any amount offered him on a horse that he cares to lay against."[liii] He frequently attempted to break the books with bets of $50,000 or more.

Regardless of Grannon's actions against them, his racetrack peers immediately recognized a threat to their livelihoods in Walbaum's banning of Grannon and drew up a petition. Every bookmaker who worked at Saratoga, except three in whose books Walbaum had an interest, signed the petition. It requested that Grannon be allowed all the track privileges he previously had enjoyed.

Faced with a general uprising of the bookmakers and a potentially huge loss of income, Walbaum realized he was in an untenable position and told Grannon he could continue to make book at Saratoga, if he so cared. "The bookmakers say that they were forced into accepting afternoon racing," the *New York Times* reported, "but that they will not be forced to make book to suit Walbaum's whims."[liv]

Under the *New York Times* headline "Judges and Stewards Who Do Not See or Ask Questions,"[lv] the issue of arranged races emerged again just days later. In the third race on August 15, 1894, a race for two-year-olds, the bay colt out of Cherry Blossom, owned by the partnership of Gideon and Daly and ridden by Griffin, was the strong favorite for the $500 purse. The strongest competition for the Cherry Blossom colt was generally considered to come from the brown filly, Miss Annie, owned by Walbaum, and ridden by Donohue.

As expected, the Cherry Blossom colt led going into the stretch run. But two other colts, Derelict and Rossmor, appeared to impede the Cherry Blossom colt's run to the finish line. The rough play forced the Cherry Blossom colt's jockey to pull up his horse at the sixteenth pole and allowed Walbaum's horse to win in an upset by three lengths.

Despite the flagrant fouling, the Cherry Blossom colt finished second by a head, ahead of Derelict. After the race the judges and stewards said nothing about the apparent fouling and failed to ask the jockeys any questions. When the Cherry Blossom colt's jockey, Griffin, made no official complaint after the race about his mount's rough treatment, Gideon severely reprimanded him.

The day after the race the *New York Times* reported, "The race had more fouling in it than would seem possible in one with so small a field of starters. But for it the Cherry Blossom colt would have won to a certainty … Honest men with open eyes are sadly needed here."[lvi] When the stewards were asked why they failed to investigate the apparent fouls on the track, they explained that the Cherry Blossom colt's jockey had acted badly at the post.

However, the race's starter, Mr. Caldwell, had not filed a complaint against the Cherry Blossom colt or the jockey. The *New York Times* reporter wrote that Derelict and Rossmor "certainly fouled the Cherry Blossom colt twice each, and made Griffin pull him up squarely when but a sixteenth of a mile from the finish, and every one but the occupants of the judges' stand saw it very plainly."[lvii]

The continuing suspicious circumstances surrounding racing at Saratoga under Walbaum's management, combined with the blatant attempt to prevent the Cherry Blossom colt from winning the race the previous day, was the last straw for many track insiders and observers. The *New York Times* reported the mounting anger and frustration led to an extraordinary plan by the Saratoga townspeople to build a rival track farther out from the town's limits in hopes that Walbaum would be forced to sell his interests in the current track.[lviii]

While Walbaum may not have made a good impression with the racing public and townsfolk, he left a lasting legacy of a different type. Under his management a new grandstand was constructed. The grandstand opened on July 25, 1892, comfortably seating 5,000 patrons and featuring a visually pleasing slate roof.

At the rear of the grandstand was the notorious Walbaum construction — the bookmaker's operation for women and children. These "retiring rooms" featured some amenities such as trimming with natural wood[lix] and telephone connections to the main ring.

At the eastern end of the grandstand, Walbaum had constructed a paved and covered betting pavilion. It comprised a circle of stalls, or cages, in which the bookmakers, their "sheetwriters," and the payoff men worked. Each stall was marked by the name of the bookmaking tenant, and below each name was a blackboard that listed the entries for the races and the odds.

The betting pavilion quickly produced a carnival-like atmosphere. The bookmakers shouted into the crowd, bid against each other for business, and provided different colored paper and printing designs for each race. The bookies also walked through the betting ring with gambling tickets and cash sticking out of their pockets, attempting to drum up new business.

When Walbaum's critics learned who had bought the track at Saratoga, they had predicted an invasion of the very worst element. Walbaum's behavior and management style almost appeared designed to vindicate his critics as bookmakers, gamblers, and plungers began flocking there for each racing season.

CHAPTER 8

The Wickedest Spot

In the 1890s America's most famous reporter, Nellie Bly (Elizabeth Cochrane), had drawn worldwide attention by traveling around the world in a record-setting seventy-two days, six hours, and ten minutes. Then *New York World* sent the famous world traveler to Saratoga. She reported, "Saratoga is the wickedest spot in the United States. Crime is holding a convention there and vice is enjoying a revival such as it never dared approach before."[i]

Bly also indignantly noted that men were known to leave their wives on the verandas to talk to actresses or to other women of questionable character, and "men of no standing and bad morals"[ii] talked to pretty girls no more than ten to fifteen years old.

At the track, she reported, admission was only $2 and gamblers, horse owners, jockeys, millionaires, and actors mingled openly. In the stands she noticed a group of "painted faces and penciled, inviting eyes,"[iii] and two boys as young as eight and ten talking about what horses they would "play" while their sisters made up pools with their mother for 25 cents.[iv] Also, Bly informed the nation of Walbaum's betting room for women and children.

Bly couldn't be blamed for her succinct description of Saratoga's gambling scene, given the number of bookmakers

John Cavanagh

and professional gamblers that invaded the town for the race meet. In 1901 a special train — the *Cavanagh Special* — began making runs from New York City to Saratoga. It usually arrived the day before the racing season started, then left two to three hours after the meeting's final race. It consisted of as many as eight cars jammed with the day's pre-eminent bookmakers and their assistants.

The more affluent bookies rode in Pullman cars while others rode in diners and day coaches. The train became an instant success at Saratoga and was eagerly anticipated. When the train arrived, the bookmakers and their assistants, accompanied by a marching band, paraded through town to their destinations, usually the best hotels in Saratoga. The train was named for its organizer, New York City bookmaker John C. "Irish John" Cavanagh.

Cavanagh had been a leading bookmaker in New York City for years and the arbiter of the betting ring since 1897. Bookmakers generally shunned publicity because they couldn't afford to allow their disputes to become public knowledge. To avoid unnecessary and possibly damaging publicity, they decided among themselves that an arbiter should be appointed to settle internal disputes.

Cavanagh also was president of the Metropolitan Turf Association, a trade organization of the bookies with the strongest financial and political backing. Members were known as "Mets"[v] and regularly pre-empted the best spots for betting at the track, handled bets at all New York state racetracks, and almost controlled gambling on horse racing in New York.

Because the members tended to exercise great control on New York horse racing, they wore distinctive buttons that usually guaranteed a higher class of bet and bettor for its wearer. The buttons, sold in much the same way as seats on the stock exchange, were not inexpensive. Memberships sold for more than they did on the stock exchange, and one purchaser, Caesar Young, is believed to have paid the highest price ever for a button, $7,000.

Many bookmakers believed that their functions were little different than Wall Street brokers, and some advertised in leading papers, sometimes in the front pages next to ads for the leading banking houses. As many as sixty bookies gathered regularly at Saratoga, where they paid as much as $100 daily for the privilege of doing business and competing against each other.

At the track the bookmakers plied their trade in the betting rings, a circle of stalls that housed them; their "sheet writers," who monitored competitors' odds and advised bookies of the risk in odds changes; and the payoff men. Each stall bore the

Bookmakers and the betting ring at Saratoga

name of the bookmaker tenant and a blackboard with the entries of upcoming races, the odds written in chalk. For each race, the bookmakers used tickets of different-colored paper and printing designs that included their business names, a ticket number, and the bet that the sheet writers inscribed in indelible ink.

Probably the most prominent bookmaker of the time was Bill Cowan, considered by his peers to be a mathematical genius. He was backed financially at one point by New York sportsman Robert H. Davis, part owner of the Boston Braves when the team won the 1914 baseball championship. While Cowan may have been clever with other people's numbers, he apparently was not always so adept at figuring his own odds. He reportedly came to Saratoga for a month after losing $250,000 on other New York tracks, won $750,000 at Saratoga, then lost it all at Belmont. Still, he died a rich man.

Two other bookmakers, Joe Ullman and Kid Weller, formed a partnership for several years that came to be known as "the Big Store,"[vi] with money they had borrowed from multimillionaire John Warner Gates. They were very successful at Saratoga and were known to take almost any bet.

Big Louis Cella, Sam Adler, and Cap Tilles controlled a syndicate known as the C.A.T. Combination. They moved to the East Coast from their headquarters in St. Louis when Governor Folk ordered the Missouri tracks closed in 1905 and at one time operated ten different books.

There also was the precocious fifteen-year-old George Shannon, who strolled through the betting ring with a $2,000 commission from the wealthy owner he represented.[vii]

The professional gamblers frequenting Saratoga at this time included the very successful, but short-tempered, Virginia Carroll, who was known to shred $10 bills and cast the torn cash at cashiers if the results were not to his liking. Carroll was also infamous for his foul mouth and was said to rival Walbaum

in his use of obscenities.[viii]

Perhaps the most successful gambler to frequent Saratoga was George E. Smith, a thin and ascetic-looking man. Cool, unemotional, and fearless, Smith was known to have never welshed on a bet. Smith had originally learned a trade as a cork cutter, but he became nationally recognized through the name he signed on betting slips, Pittsburgh Phil, when he began playing the races at poolrooms in Pittsburgh.

Pittsburgh Phil (left)

At the height of his career, Pittsburgh Phil maintained an organization that spent $1,000 per day to obtain inside information from jockeys, stable managers, grooms, trainers, and private clockers. He was so successful that bookies had agents trail him in the hope of obtaining information that would enable them to cut the price on any horse he favored. Bill Cowan ruefully admitted he paid more money to Pittsburgh Phil than to any other big Turf gambler because Pittsburgh Phil was so adept at his trade.

Even on his deathbed, at the age of forty-three in a tuberculosis sanatorium, Pittsburgh Phil tried to game the odds and asked his doctor, "How long will I live?" The doctor told him twenty-four hours. Pittsburgh Phil then managed to coax his doctor into a $10,000 bet that the gambler would live longer, and each wrote out a check for the wager. Twenty-four-and-a-half hours later, Pittsburgh Phil died, clutching the doctor's check in his hand.

While the bookies feared expert gamblers such as Pittsburgh

Marcus Daly

Phil, their natural adversaries were the plungers, the set of very wealthy men who regularly gambled such large sums of money they could put the bookies out of business.

One notorious plunger was horse owner Marcus Daly, otherwise known as the "Copper King." Daly, who owned Bitter Root Stud in Montana, had made his money when he purchased a small silver mine known as the Anaconda, which happened to contain a huge quantity of copper. Daly was known to be generous and fair with his employees, and while he was in charge of the Anaconda Mining Company, there was no labor unrest.

But Daly was also a ruthless gambling competitor. In 1896 Daly came close to breaking the New York bookies with his horse Ogden. Ogden had secretly trained at Saratoga before winning the Futurity at Sheepshead Bay. Daly won as much as $1 million from the New York bookies,[ix] and had there not been a miscommunication in the placing of the bet, Daly might have won five times that amount and probably broken the bookies.

But the dominant plunger of the day may have been the gruff John Warner Gates. By the time he was thirty, Gates, a tall, stout man from the Midwest with a heavy mustache, had made a fortune selling barbed wire to cattle ranchers in Texas. With his fortune, the shrewd and daring Gates became an active player in the stock market and was known to have created mammoth trusts, upset the financial markets, and precipitated panics.

At one point he controlled the Louisville and Nashville Railroad before selling his interest to J. Pierpont Morgan. Gates also had been an integral part of the formation of the billion-dollar U.S. Steel Corporation but had so offended Morgan with a questionable deal that a wildly angry Morgan bought him out for $1 million.

Gates was a flamboyant man whom intimates referred to as "the Big Stiff."[x] During the summers he usually disdained vests so as to show off the three diamonds sparkling from his shirt, along with the diamonds on his suspenders. Because he loved to gamble, he would forego sleep to wager immense sums of money in marathon gambling sessions that lasted for two to three days and from which he probably earned his other nickname "Bet-a-Million." It didn't matter to him whether he gambled on cards, horses, or, in one infamous incident, the progress of raindrops down a windowpane.

The ruthless Gates saw little difference in investing or gambling, thrived on high-stakes situations, and posed a threat

Ogden provided a betting coup for owner Marcus Daly

to the various gaming establishments because he had vast financial resources and used his wealth to win. What mattered most to Gates was the thrill of gambling; the higher the stakes, the more he loved it. Even in a time when a dozen bookies could accept a $50,000 bet, his wagers were extraordinary. As such, Gates presented a real danger to the professional gamblers and bookmakers in the betting ring. They knew men like Gates easily had the resources and the will to put them out of business, if luck was on his side.

Gates was a regular at Saratoga, and while at Saratoga, Gates and his friend and fellow gambler John A. Drake lived in adjoining cottages at the United States Hotel. Drake, who had inherited great wealth, raced Thoroughbreds including the Futurity winner Savable. It was generally believed at the time that Gates had a half interest in the stable as the two were at the track together daily.

On one afternoon in August 1902, when Gates and Drake were at the track, Gates lost $400,000, then accompanied some guests to dinner at Morrissey's old casino, where he promptly located the faro table in the main gaming room. Playing the ordinary limits of $400 and $1,000, Gates quickly lost another $25,000. Gates then moved upstairs to one of the private rooms where the limits were set at $2,500 on cases and $5,000 on doubles. By 10 p.m. he was down $150,000.

Refusing to bear the loss, Gates sought out the casino manager, Richard Canfield, and requested a higher limit. Canfield calmly listened to Gates, who was puffing on a cigar, and inquired about the present limit and the requested limit. Gates said he wanted to double both limits; Canfield considered and then agreed. Canfield then stepped toward the door, stopped, turned around, and said, "Are you sure that's enough?"[xi]

Gates deemed the new limits to be sufficient and returned to the table for one of the biggest faro games on record. From

10 p.m. until dawn, Gates bet from $5,000 to $10,000 on every turn of the cards. By midnight his luck had turned, despite four dealers working in relays, and by 2 a.m. he was even again. His string of luck continued and by dawn he was up $150,000, a sum that cut his total losses for the day from more than $500,000 to $250,000.

W.C. Whitney (left) and August Belmont II

Whether it was the result of that night or another day at the track, Gates' gambling antics drew the attention of August Belmont II, the chairman of The Jockey Club. Belmont told Gates that he feared his gambling would stir up anti-gambling activists and asked, "Why don't you limit your bets to $10,000?"[xii] Gates refused and said, "I think no man should bet unless he's sure he's right. And when he's sure he's right, he should be willing to bet every dollar he owns. That's the way I bet. For me, there's no fun in betting just a few thousand. I want to lay down enough to hurt the other fellow if he loses and enough for me if I lose."[xiii]

That same month in 1902 Gates almost succeeded in breaking several bookmakers at Saratoga's betting ring. He entered the ring with $50,000, with the intention to bet it all on High Chancellor in the fourth race. Gates bet $10,000 at 12-10 odds with the first bookmaker and then moved to another. But by the time he reached the second bookmaker, the odds had fallen to no better than even money.

Despite the decreasing odds Gates persisted in betting the entire $50,000. When the race was over, his horse was the

The Saratoga paddock in the early 1900s

winner, and Gates $50,000 richer. The Big Stiff then made a point of strolling among the disgruntled bookmakers and their assistants in the crowded betting ring before exiting, accompanied by a large hired servant pushing a wheelbarrow stuffed with Gates' winnings.[xiv]

◆◆◆

The Walbaum years also resulted in another notable arrival. William Collins Whitney, an attorney from New York City, was the son of a public-spirited Massachusetts family and was well connected by marriage. Whitney had married Flora Payne, the sister of Yale chum Oliver Hazard Payne, who was to become the treasurer of Standard Oil.

Whitney, involved in New York City politics as a Reform Democrat, made a name for himself and later became a lawyer for New York City. In that role, he battled the corrupt Boss Tweed in Tweed's final desperate days and is credited with reforming the city's law department. At a time of rampant corruption in the management of the city, the *New York Times* noted Whitney's work at the city law department was "marked by vigor and economy."[xv]

Whitney then became involved in state and national politics when he helped elect Grover Cleveland governor. When Cleveland became president, he appointed Whitney secretary of the Navy. Whitney later ran Cleveland's successful 1892 presidential re-election campaign.

Whitney's career in the private sector also was marked with success. He became director of the New York Cable Rail Company and a permanent partner with founder Thomas Fortune Ryan. Ryan and Whitney then created the Metropolitan Street Railway Company and swallowed up several cable and electric railway companies. They then forged an alliance with Peter A.B. Widener, Philadelphia's street railway king, and battled Jay Gould, who controlled the elevated railways in Philadelphia. By the end of 1900, Ryan and Whitney controlled nearly all of the street railways in Manhattan and the Bronx.

Successful and politically connected, Whitney appeared to be in control of his destiny when tragedy struck: His wife Flora died in 1893. In the wake of the personal tragedy, Whitney decided to pursue some longtime interests. He had always retained an interest in breeding horses and the Turf and wanted to find a way to defeat his Wall Street rival, James R. Keene, a noted breeder and owner of racehorses.

Keene had made a fortune speculating in mining and railroad stocks in San Francisco. He was also an aggressive speculator and in 1884 had attempted to corner the Chicago wheat market, an endeavor during which he butted heads with Jay Gould and was destroyed financially. But Keene, who lived for the thrill of the deal, bounced back and became one of America's most sensational brokers. Within six years he was back on the market and with William Havemayer, helped control the sugar market.

During his long career in the stock market, Keene made, lost, and regained fortunes. He was known as an aggressive player who manipulated the stocks "as a fierce game to be played as a sporting proposition, and without any quarter whatever to others engaged in it."[xvi]

Keene had joined William Collins Whitney and Thomas Fortune Ryan in a move to control a significant share of American Tobacco stock. Before the deal could be consummated, however, Keene defected and sold his share to Oliver Payne, Whitney's former brother-in-law turned enemy. Whitney never forgave Keene, and they became bitter rivals.

Whitney had company. With his market manipulations, Keene had made some other very powerful enemies, including Gould. When Keene moved to the East Coast, Gould warned unabashedly, "Keene came east in a private car. I'll send him back in a box car."[xvii]

Determined to pursue his Turf interests and perhaps his rivalry with Keene, Whitney became a charter member of The Jockey Club in 1894. Then he followed the lead of good friend Thomas Hitchcock, who had a residence, stable, and private track in Aiken, South Carolina. Whitney also built a mansion, stable, and a mile track there.

Whitney asked successful owner-trainer Sam Hildreth to train horses for him. In 1898 Whitney bought Hildreth's stable and made Hildreth trainer, while contracting with owner-trainer John Madden as a consultant. That year Whitney's horses won twenty-five races and earned more than $38,000. The next year he had twenty-seven horses in his stable and won thirty-two races, earning $61,550. In 1900 he entered Ballyhoo Bey in the Futurity and targeted Keene's entries. Ballyhoo Bey won $33,580 and defeated Keene's favored trio of Olympian, Tommy Atkins, and Cap and Bells.

Whitney also backed a plan by New York banker and longtime Saratoga regular Richard T. Wilson Jr. to buy Walbaum's interest in the track. For several years no one had been listed in the guide as president of the Saratoga Association — it only listed C.F. Ruh Jr. as the secretary. In December 1901 the deal was made, and Walbaum was given $365,000 for the track. Whitney was elected president; Andrew Miller, a prominent New Yorker and one of the founders of *Life* magazine,[xviii] was designated secretary and treasurer, and a new name was unveiled — the Saratoga Association for the Improvement of the Breed of Horses. That same year The Jockey Club — including chairman August Belmont II, Francis Hitchcock, who was the New York Jockey Club steward,[xix] and the club's other stewards — had convened its first formal meeting at the track. In addition, Horse Haven, the training facility across Union Avenue from the racetrack, was enlarged to handle the selling of Thoroughbreds at public auction.

The idea for an annual yearling sale "of the great breeding establishments of Kentucky, Tennessee, and California"[xx] was immediately accepted by major owners and breeders. The Saratoga Association funded the project and planned stables to house nine hundred yearlings and a three-quarters-mile straightaway for breaking and training. The stalls were let to breeding and auction companies, and buyers were allowed after the summer meeting to exercise their horses on the racecourse and the training tracks. Whitney later paid $40,000 for the land surrounding, but not including, Horse Haven, that was to become a one-mile track, nicknamed "Oklahoma," supposedly because the walk to it took as long as a walk to the state.

Whitney also implemented several changes to revitalize the racetrack program. For the 1902 meet, he reinstated several races that had disappeared under Walbaum and offered more significant rewards for winning entries. For the opening race, the Saratoga Handicap, a $10,000 award was offered to the winner. The Saratoga Special, a winner-take-all for two-year-olds, was added and was worth $14,500 and a $500 silver cup. The Travers Stakes was reintroduced to the program and offered $6,750 to the winner.

When the gates opened for the first day of the 1902 racing season, 9,000 people showed up and were introduced to a renovated plant, designed by New York architect Charles Leavitt at a cost of at least $1 million. The renovations included an increase in the grandstand capacity from 5,000 to 6,000; an enlarged betting ring; a track lengthened from a mile to a mile and one-eighth and widened to one hundred feet except for the sixty-five-foot second turn. Other renovations included a larger saddling paddock with twenty-five stalls; a cottage for the jockeys, clerk of scales, and other track officials; another field stand west of the clubhouse; and stables for 370 horses.

For the increased admission price of $3 (up from $2), the fans watched a re-energized program of six races that made racing fun again at Saratoga.

CHAPTER 9

Sysonby

In 1902 Optime, a daughter of English Triple Crown winner Ormonde, was shipped from England to New York City and sold at auction, where James R. Keene paid $6,600 for her. Very soon after her purchase, Optime gave birth to a smallish colt by Epsom Derby winner Melton. A groom, Ernest Shackleford, later described the foal as "a common, cheap-looking, lop-eared colt."[i]

Nothing came easy for the ungainly colt — he was short and apparently slow. In 1903 Keene was unconvinced of the colt's worth and resolved to sell him. A handicapper inspecting the colt before the sale observed the muscular neck, massive body, and huge stride and said that the youngster was destined to become a racehorse "with which no horse could contend."[ii]

Keene's son, Foxhall, took the words to heart and wisely interceded before the colt was sold. Foxhall named the awkward colt Sysonby after his English hunting lodge. The next year James Keene was still determined to dispatch the ungainly colt and scheduled Sysonby to be sent to England.

But Keene's trainer James R. Rowe, who knew something about quality horses, intervened. Determined to prevent the colt from slipping away, Rowe brought the colt out in blankets

Sysonby's Flash Stakes

and bandages for Keene's inspection. The trainer moaned and groaned about the colt's fragile health and told Keene he feared for Sysonby's safety on a long voyage. Rowe then told Keene that Sysonby obviously needed to stay where he was.

Keene relented and decided to race Sysonby with his American stable. Foxhall Keene's and Rowe's faith in the ungainly colt would be rewarded when Sysonby developed into one of the most dominant racehorses of the twentieth century.

The two-year-old Sysonby arrived at Saratoga in the summer of 1904 off of two much-talked-about victories at Brighton Beach. The colt had debuted at Brighton Beach, winning a five-and-a-half-furlong maiden by six lengths. Just two days later he had won the Brighton Junior Stakes by four lengths.

At Saratoga, Sysonby was entered in the five-and-a-half-furlong Flash Stakes on August 1. The four-horse field included another of note, Sysonby's stablemate Augur, who carried 119 pounds to Sysonby's 125. The two were co-favored at 2-5. Next choice among the gamblers was L.V. Bell's Glorifier, who also carried 125 pounds, at 11-5. The other entrant, Sidney Paget's 40-1 longshot Trapper, carried 117 pounds.

It was an easy win for Sysonby, but not quite so easy for his jockey, who from start to finish "was striving his utmost to keep him back within a reasonable distance of his field, but he found it more of a task than he bargained for."[iii] Keene's colt was "so full of run"[iv] that he would have none of his jockey's attempts

James Keene

to restrain him, and he broke away from the other horses with a tremendous burst of speed.

Sysonby led all the way to take the Flash by six lengths in 1:06 4/5 and was followed by Augur, who earlier trailed Glorifier but made a rush at the end to finish second. Glorifier showed some speed but, after an attempt to stay with Sysonby, tired in the stretch. Trapper stayed close for half of the race but then fell away.

Immediately after the race, the winning colt garnered a large crowd, including legendary horseman John E. Madden. Speaking with owner Keene, Madden said, "When I saw Sysonby work at Brighton Beach, Mr. Keene, I sold out my colts. He is a great colt, and I made up my mind my colts had no chance to beat him."[v]

After the race Keene said he believed that his colt was even faster than "Domino in his best days."[vi] Apparently others shared his opinion, and Keene commented on an offer to purchase his star. Keene stated that Andrew Miller had approached him and said, "If you wish to sell the colt, Mr. Keene, I can get you a purchaser at $100,000."[vii]

Keene declined the offer and declared the colt not for sale. While the offer to purchase Sysonby had been made anonymously, the Chicago *Daily Tribune* correspondent wrote, "It is believed that W.B. Leeds wanted the colt."[viii] With a potential superstar on his hands, Keene probably was loathe to admit that he hadn't wanted to keep the colt at first.

Sysonby had made a fairly emphatic statement about his ability with his first three starts. Next up was the five-and-a-half-furlong Saratoga Special, and the cheap-looking, lop-eared colt already was starting to scare away the competition with his matchless burst of speed.

Only two other horses appeared at the post for the Special with a stake worth $14,000, in front of a crowd that was described as "the largest crowd ever seen at the Saratoga racecourse."[ix] Both were decided underdogs. John E. Madden's Hot Shot carried 120 pounds and was at odds of 20-1; John A. Drake's Britisher was listed at 15-1.

Unlike in the Flash Stakes, Sysonby was caught flat footed at the start and found himself nearly a length behind. His alarmed fans jumped to their feet as Keene's sensational colt was "not as quick to get to his stride as usual."[x]

Within fifty yards from the start, however, Sysonby was in full stride, much to his fans' relief. To catch and pass Hot Shot and Britisher, Sysonby ran the first furlong in :11 1/5, the quarter in :22 3/5, and the three-eighths in :34 1/5.[xi]

With a lead of two lengths over Britisher, and the race in hand, Sysonby cantered home in 1:07, finishing six lengths ahead of Hot Shot, who had passed Britisher in the stretch. Even with a terrible start, Sysonby used his speed to overwhelm the competition, and his time shattered by one and one-fifth seconds the race record held by Goldsmith and Irish Lad.

Unlike many of his rivals in the Turf, Keene had actually worked with horses, as a horse tender at Fort Reading, and had learned to love horses.[xii] While he had misjudged Sysonby, Keene wasn't in the habit of making many mistakes in the Turf business. On the same day that Sysonby won the $14,000 Special, Keene's Delhi won the Great Republic Stakes, yielding winnings for the day of $56,000 and putting Keene's stable atop the leading owners' list with a total of $135,000.[xiii]

Sysonby's three-year-old season went much the same way as his first four starts at two had. He won, usually in a convincing manner. He was undefeated in six starts on the year when he was shipped to Saratoga for the August 12 Great Republic Stakes.

In fact, the only blemish on Sysonby's career had been the 1904 Futurity, in which he had finished a struggling third to the talented filly Artful and the undefeated Tradition. After the race Foxhall Keene claimed a groom had drugged Sysonby. Inquiries were made, and later one of Keene's grooms admitted taking a bribe to drug Sysonby. It had become apparent that the once-

Sysonby dead heats with Race King in the Metropolitan

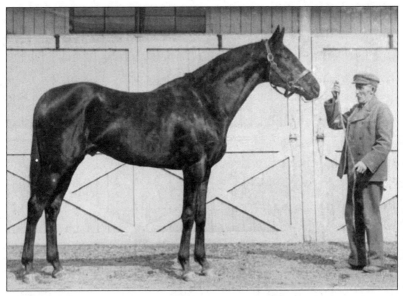

Oiseau

deemed expendable Sysonby had the heart of a champion. Even a tranquilizer-induced stupor couldn't prevent Sysonby from finishing in the money against talented competition.

For the 1905 season Sysonby returned for the inaugural meeting at the brand new Belmont Park on Long Island and finished first in a dead heat with Race King in the Metropolitan Handicap. After that it was a steady string of solo victories: Tidal, Commonwealth, Lawrence Realization, Iroquois, Brighton Derby.

Coming into the Great Republic Stakes, many track observers and insiders believed that Diamond Jim Brady's Canadian champion Oiseau would at last present a credible test for Keene's phenom.

While Sysonby had displayed tremendous bursts of speed, and clearly possessed the will to win, he would have his hands full defeating Oiseau, who had won eight stakes races in 1904[xiv] as a two-year-old, including the six-furlong Bashford Manor Stakes at Churchill Downs,[xv] and the mile Champagne Stakes at Belmont.[xvi]

Oiseau had been bred by Joseph Warner near his nursery outside of Nashville. As a juvenile, Oiseau had won fourteen of his eighteen starts and was considered the best horse ever bred in Tennessee.[xvii]

Oiseau's performances were so strong that some Turf observers believed Oiseau could even challenge for the three-year-old championship. The colt had been so impressive that a Mr. Matt Allen had "made a handsome offer"[xviii] for Oiseau. The owners, John G. Greener & Co, refused the initial offer, but a second offer from Allen was accepted in October 1904. While the exact sum was never made public, the owners accepted an amount that was confirmed by their representative to be close to $50,000.[xix]

Weeks later James Buchanan "Diamond Jim" Brady purchased Oiseau from Allen, specifically to try and win the Great Republic Stakes. Oiseau began the 1905 season strong with wins that included the Swift and the Spendrift stakes. Coming into the Great Republic, oddsmakers listed Oiseau as the second choice at 18-5.

As the race approached, there were many reasons to consider Oiseau a worthy challenger for Sysonby. In addition to his outstanding record, Oiseau had great bloodlines. He was sired by Ornus, who in turn had been sired by the great English Thoroughbred Bend Or. Also, reports circulated around the track that in the weeks prior to the big race, Oiseau had "worked fast and that he had a good chance to beat Sysonby."[xx] Also, the two had met once before and neither had won. Finally, Oiseau was to be ridden by Mr. Redfern, an experienced and capable jockey.

As impressive as his colt was, it was hard to overlook Oiseau's owner, James Buchanan "Diamond Jim" Brady. For years Brady had been a prominent figure on Broadway, the theatre district,

Diamond Jim Brady

where he was a regular at the Bijou, and first saw Lillian Russell, the up-and-coming actress during the 1881-82 season. He soon introduced himself and they became fast friends.

Brady stood more than six feet tall, weighed 250 pounds, and savored the good life with every fiber of his large body. Known for his hearty appetite, Brady was a regular at two of New York's fancier restaurants, Delmonico's and Sherry's. A typical lunch for Brady consisted of two lobsters, deviled crabs, clams, oysters, and beef, followed by several whole pies.[xxi]

What Diamond Jim lacked in education and polite manners, he made up for with charm, determination, and a flair for self-promotion. By the time he was forty years old, Brady was worth $12 million and earned another $1 million every year from his sales job with the railroads. With his growing wealth, he accumulated thirty sets of jewels, consisting of more than 20,000 diamonds of various sizes and cuts and 6,000 other precious stones. Each day of the month he wore a different set of gems. He wore the jewels on just about every piece of clothing imaginable: collar buttons, shirt studs, cufflinks, necktie pins, and belt buckles. He even had diamond-studded pencils and underwear. (Thus his nickname Diamond Jim.)

New York restaurateur George Rector offered the following description: "When Diamond Jim had all his illumination in place, he looked like an excursion steamer at twilight." On one occasion Rector teased Diamond Jim for the jewelry display, and Brady replied, "Them as has 'em wears 'em."[xxii]

When he wasn't entertaining the railroad men with lavish parties, Diamond Jim could often be seen in Saratoga in the company of Russell, who had become one of America's most admired women. Diamond Jim had become a regular companion of the transplanted Iowan with the beautiful curves, golden hair, and creamy complexion since he first saw her on a stage in New York City.

Lillian Russell

Diamond Jim also gambled on the horses. At the races a scene almost as riveting as the struggles on the track unfolded regularly when the large and animated Diamond Jim jumped up and down while issuing incomprehensible guttural sounds as he cheered his horses on.

His interest in the horses had led to ownership. One spring night in 1901 in the Waldorf Astoria bar, the Dwyer brothers, who had taken a beating in the stock market, approached Diamond Jim. They quickly needed to raise some cash and inquired whether Diamond Jim was interested in buying some of their Thoroughbreds. Diamond Jim agreed, bought two of their horses, and decided to race them as a silent partner with an agreeable friend, F.C. McLewee.

When his newly acquired horses, Gold Heels and Major Daingerfield, proved successful, rumors swirled in the racing world that somehow Diamond Jim had rigged the contests. Some horsemen didn't like the flamboyant Diamond Jim, and

Sysonby warming up at Saratoga

in 1902 The Jockey Club passed a new rule forbidding silent partnerships. Rather than take the chance that his interest in racing would offend some of his customers, Diamond Jim sold the horses. In late 1904, however, he bought into racing again with the purchase of Oiseau.

At the time, the one-and-a-quarter-mile Great Republic was the highlight race of the Saratoga season and offered a lucrative purse of $50,000. At least 20,000 people jammed the stands and filed onto the infield to watch Sysonby face off against Oiseau and three others, including Broomstick, a son of 1896 Kentucky Derby winner Ben Brush.

Betting was heavy by the large crowd, which expected a terrific race, and Sysonby was favored at 2-5. Even Congress Park casino owner Richard Canfield, who rarely was seen at the track and was known to gamble infrequently if at all on the races, appeared at the track, and word spread quickly that Canfield had bet $30,000 on Oiseau.

Up against stiff competition with a horse primed to break his undefeated string, Sysonby could not have had a worse start. He was turned sideways when the barrier lifted, and by the time he got straightened and headed in the proper direction, the other horses were well down the track.

While Sysonby struggled at the start, Oiseau was "away flying"[xxiii] and led for the first three furlongs. Only Sysonby's blazing speed prevented a disaster. After a quarter-mile Oiseau had a one-length lead over Prince Hamburg and Dandelion, but Sysonby was rapidly closing on them. Broomstick trailed the field.

Onlookers in the grandstand jumped out of their seats while those on the crowded lawn stood and watched in amazement as Sysonby ran the first three furlongs on a curve in :32 4/5, a feat unmatched for years, and caught the other horses. At the half-mile post he blew past Oiseau so quickly that Oiseau appeared "that he had broken down"[xxiv] and surged to a two-length lead. At that point, while still far from the finish, everyone could sense that Sysonby simply would not be denied.

Oiseau was still in second and led Broomstick by at least six lengths, but the pace set by Sysonby had virtually eliminated Dandelion and Prince Hamburg from the race. Coming to the head of the stretch, Sysonby increased his lead to five lengths as the overmatched but determined Oiseau hung on. The crowd was almost beside itself and the "turf enthusiasts in the clubhouse and grandstand arose en masse."[xxv] Many men jubilantly threw their hats and canes into the air, and women waved their handkerchiefs.

At the finish it was Sysonby by three lengths in a time of 2:07. Despite his struggles at the barrier, Sysonby finished only one and one-fifth seconds off the previous year's winning time. Oiseau ended up second, a length in front of Broomstick, with the other two trailing badly behind.

Many fans were disappointed in Oiseau's performance, but

Sysonby's Great Republic Stakes

while he led in the race for the first half-mile the pace had been extremely fast. After Sysonby took the lead and Sysonby's jockey realized that none of the other horses could challenge, the pace slowed considerably and the mile was finished in 1:39 2/5. Despite the slower pace in the second half-mile, the crowd, having sensed the inevitable victory, responded with "prolonged cheering, though the horse was far from the winning post."[xxvi]

After the race, thousands left their spots in the stands and on the lawn to file past the great champion in his stall. The excited correspondent for the *New York Times* called the race, "the greatest day ever seen at the Union Avenue Park."[xxvii]

With his victory, Sysonby passed the $100,000 mark with $151,545. His Great Republic Stakes purse placed him second on the list of the biggest money earners for the year, behind only Domino, with half the season still in front of him.[xxviii]

Sysonby's come-from-behind victory removed the last obstacle to Sysonby's dominance as a three-year-old. From Saratoga he went on to win the Century Stakes, where he again beat

Broomstick and the season's champion mare, Eugenia Burch. Sysonby then went to Sheepshead Bay for the Annual Champion Stakes, where he again defeated Oiseau and Broomstick.

Sysonby finished his three-year-old campaign undefeated, with wins at distances from a mile to two and a quarter miles. He was regarded as Horse of the Year and champion three-year-old colt and earned $184,438 in his career with a record of fourteen wins in fifteen starts.

Before he could sire any cheap-looking, lop-eared colts of his own, however, the champion Sysonby contracted variola, a liver disease, and died in his stall at Sheepshead Bay in June 1906. More than four thousand people turned out to pay their respects and watch the burial of Sysonby in front of Keene's stables. Later Sysonby's body was exhumed, and his skeleton has been on display since 1907 at the American Museum of Natural History in New York City.

CHAPTER 10

The Black Sheep

A young man with a passion for gambling, Arnold Rothstein
first arrived in Saratoga in 1904 on the *Cavanagh Special*.
He was just twenty-one years old, the son of well-to-do and
devout parents who had almost turned their backs on the young
gambler.

His Jewish grandparents had fled persecution in Russia, and
after arriving in New York, had worked hard to create a new life
and maintain the heritage of their forefathers. Arnold's father,
Abraham Rothstein, became a successful cotton-goods dealer.
He regularly attended synagogue, observed the Sabbath, and
was known to friends and associates as "Abe the Just."[i]

Abraham realized early that his ways would not be his son's
ways. One day Abraham happened upon a truly shocking scene:
He found three-year-old Arnold threateningly wielding a knife
over brother Harry as the older boy slept.

Deeply disturbed with what he saw, Abraham asked Arnold
why he would contemplate violence against his own brother.
Arnold responded abruptly, "I hate Harry."[ii]

Several years later, when his exasperated father told his
wayward son to be proud of his Jewish heritage, Arnold
shrugged, "Who cares about this stuff? This is America, not

Arnold Rothstein

Jerusalem. I'm an American. Let Harry be a Jew."[iii]

While Harry would become a well-liked and accomplished student, Arnold disdained school and fell behind in his studies. Only for math did he show any interest; in fact, he excelled. At school Arnold amazed his fellow students with his mathematical abilities, but that wasn't enough for the youth and he dropped out.

Arnold chose the famous gentleman gambler Richard Canfield, whose career he followed in the newspapers, as a role model, and the youth began to gravitate toward New York's Longacre Square, which would later become more famous as Times Square. There the young Rothstein found the gamblers whose lives he aspired to. It was a path Arnold followed all his life.

Abraham Rothstein continued to reprimand his son for choosing such a wayward pursuit, reminding him that gambling is a sin. Arnold wouldn't listen; instead, he used his father's faith against him. When Abraham removed his expensive gold watch before going to synagogue, young Arnold often grabbed the watch, raced to a pawnshop, hocked the watch, and used the money to finance gambling and loan sharking.[iv]

After Arnold left school, he worked for his father's company. But he passed his time running floating craps games, operating out of hotel suites or, infrequently, from ocean liners, and became one of the city's most famous plungers.

In 1919 Rothstein married actress Carolyn Green on his sixth trip to the Spa. On their wedding night Rothstein borrowed Carolyn's jewelry as collateral for bets. Every morning he took her to the track and then wandered off to arrange bets. At night he left her at home while he gambled at the casinos.

Rothstein liked Saratoga so much that he decided to convert one of Saratoga's grandest estates, Mr. and Mrs. George A. Shapiro's Bonnie Brook Farm, into an extravagant casino known as the Brook. The estate was on the outskirts of Saratoga and was actually a working farm with a mansion and a racing stable. Rothstein bought the majority share of the Brook with partner Nat Evans, who also was Rothstein's partner in several Long Island gambling houses and was one of Rothstein's underlings when Rothstein allegedly "fixed" the World Series.

Rothstein also was a silent partner in Saratoga's Chicago Club and several other gaming establishments. The Brook catered only to the very wealthy and offered cuisine that compared favorably with New York City's finest dining rooms. He refused to admit anyone not attired in evening clothes or not listed in the social registers.

Using underworld contacts developed in New York — men such as Waxey Gordon and Big Maxey Greenberg[v] — Rothstein developed an expansive bootlegging operation that distributed alcohol to restaurants, night clubs, and gambling clubs during Prohibition. He also introduced to Saratoga small-time hoodlums such as Jack "Legs" Diamond, Meyer Lansky, and Charles "Lucky" Luciano, men who later became infamous figures in American history.

With the help of these men, Rothstein's Brook was profitable.

Harry Sinclair

Rothstein split 56 percent of the profits with Nat Evans and men such as local bookmaker Henry Tobin and "his henchmen."[vi]

To ensure as little interference as possible, Rothstein gave 16 percent of the profits to local politicians. With the assistance of local gambler Jules Formel, who for $1,000 arranged a deal with district attorney Charles B. Andrus that allowed the Brook to open with roulette and chemin de fer tables, Andrus received $60,000 from Rothstein, and for the money Rothstein received advance knowledge of when the Brook would be raided. When the authorities raided the club, they would surprisingly see nothing to indicate gambling occurred at the club.[vii]

At the Brook, Rothstein was a graceful and charming host who had an interest in art. He also became a friend and confidant of political bosses, social elites, sports champions, stage and movie celebrities, and tycoons. One of those tycoons was Harry Sinclair. A former druggist's clerk who had become extremely rich from oil ventures, including the founding of Sinclair Oil in 1916, Sinclair was not knowledgeable about horses or horse racing but had an interest in the Turf and was willing to spend and bet large amounts of money.

Sinclair had a connection with Arnold Rothstein from the days in New York City when Rothstein ran a floating card game that moved from hotel to hotel. Sometime during the summer of 1919, Rothstein phoned Sinclair. During the conversation Sinclair agreed to bet $90,000 on the Chicago White Sox in the upcoming World Series meeting with the Cincinnati Reds.[viii]

That World Series would earn Rothstein infamy. The Reds won the championship in a stunning upset, amid accusations that someone had arranged the outcome. Later some of the Sox players confirmed that they had indeed been paid to lose (the infamous "Black Sox" scandal). Rothstein's name was mentioned, and the gambler was called to testify before a grand jury, but no evidence could verify his involvement and he was never indicted. Despite whatever losses Sinclair may have incurred on that World Series, he later became a regular at the Brook.

In 1920 Sinclair met Sam Hildreth, whose success as a trainer had propelled him to the upper echelon of racing society, training for the likes of Lucky Baldwin, W.C. Whitney, and August Belmont II. From childhood Hildreth had had a passion for gambling. There seemed to be no game he wouldn't try, and for years he was one of the biggest faro players in the country. He also liked to gamble on the horses and was even rumored to be a plunger. Hildreth was so good at playing the horses that in 1889 when he ran up a string of wins at Gottfried Walbaum's Guttenberg track, the bookies hesitated to take his bets and gave him terrible odds.

Around the time Sinclair met Hildreth, Rothstein decided to try his own hand at racing. He established Redstone (Roth = red, stein = stone) Stable to breed and race (and bet on) quality runners.

Hildreth and Rothstein had been friends for some time, and Hildreth had helped

Sam Hildreth

Rothstein succeed at the track and profit from huge gambling payoffs. Their first big payoff had occurred in 1917.

In 1917 Hildreth trained Hourless for August Belmont and had been particularly upset about his horse's loss to Wilfred Vian's English-born chestnut colt, Omar Khayyam, in the Lawrence Realization Stakes at Belmont Park in October. Hildreth had watched in frustration as Hourless' jockey lost his whip at the break, then hand-rode the colt to an almost certain win, when almost inexplicably Hourless was "pocketed"[ix] between the rail and Omar Khayyam in the run down the stretch.

Although Omar Khayyam was a quality Thoroughbred having won the 1917 Kentucky Derby and the Travers at Saratoga, Hildreth had been sure his horse was the better runner. Immediately after the race Hildreth had asked the management at Laurel Park in Baltimore to set up a mile and a quarter duel between Hourless and Omar Khayyam.

The Laurel management agreed and organized a race for the right to claim the unofficial title of "three-year-old of the year," a $10,000 prize for the winner, and a gold cup donated by *Washington Post* publisher Edward B. McLean.

The day before the October 18 race Hourless was established as a 3-4 favorite, and Arnold Rothstein reveled in the opportunity to make a lot of money on the race. Rothstein attempted to bet $240,000 against $100,000 at that price but could find no takers for a bet that size.[x] However, Rothstein left word he was still looking for a high-stakes bet and retired to bed hopeful of a taker.

Receiving a call from a Baltimore bookmaker the next morning, Rothstein was told a syndicate was ready to book any bet he might make, without limits. Rothstein, who was not a trusting sort by nature, was suspicious of the offer to bet without limit and wondered whether some kind of fix was in on the race or whether the Baltimore gamblers perhaps had information on Hourless' condition unknown to the public.

Omar Khayyam

A concerned Rothstein then sent some members of his entourage to the track where they listened to the racetrack gossip and checked on the condition of Hourless. Both the stableman who walked the horse that morning and the groom who accompanied them attested to Hourless' good health.

For Rothstein that meant the Baltimore gamblers had some kind of inside knowledge about the race or had made some kind of a deal with someone associated with it. Rothstein checked with Hourless' owner, August Belmont II, and the owner knew of nothing inappropriate.

Because Rothstein had booked some of the very large bets that Hildreth had made on his horse, he knew that the trainer was making this race a matter of personal pride. So Rothstein phoned Hildreth.

The generally accepted version of this conversation at that time was circulated by *New York Sun* reporter Edwin Hill. Hill reported that Rothstein had called and said, "Mr. Hildreth, you don't know me, but my name is Arnold Rothstein and I am a gambler. I am not asking anything from you, of course, but I have something to tell you that you ought to know, not only in the interest of Mr. Belmont, but in the interest of racing."[xi]

Hill's version of the conversation had Hildreth listening to Rothstein, thanking him, but offering no information before hanging up. Then Rothstein called the Baltimore bookmaker and told the bookmaker that he would agree to the bet on Hourless and wager $400,000 to $300,000 to win.

Later that day Hildreth continued his silence until ten minutes before the horses went to the post. Then without notice, Hildreth asked Frankie Robinson, a young and relatively inexperienced jockey who had been riding Harry Payne Whitney's horses, to ride Hourless in the race, instead of Hourless' regular jockey, Jimmy Butwell.

With Robinson's name posted instead of Butwell's, the crowd was startled and the gamblers at the track stunned. But in front of 20,000 people, Hourless, with Robinson on top, set a world record of 2:02 for the distance and won by a length. Rothstein won $300,000 from his wager.

Later it turned out that Hill's assertion that Rothstein and Hildreth spoke before the race had been accurate. But Hill's version was missing several key facts: 1) Rothstein and Hildreth had known each other for years; 2) Rothstein and Hildreth had a history of gambling together; 3) Hildreth knew that Rothstein had the best information on racing in the gambling world; and 4) Rothstein's wife, Carolyn, who had traveled to Baltimore for the race, later repeated what Rothstein had told her regarding his conversation with Hildreth, "I told Sam the word was out that his horse was going to lose unless he made some changes. He told me he would make them."[xii]

The growing relationship between the two gamblers was both friendly and financial. It was a connection that had proven to be mutually profitable, and it would again, at Saratoga's 1921 Travers Stakes, with even higher stakes in play.

Hourless

Harry Payne Whitney's outstanding filly Prudery was the only horse entered that year for the Travers until Rothstein entered his Fair Play colt, Sporting Blood. Sporting Blood was a good runner but not in the same class as Prudery, who had recently won the Alabama. Prudery was just one of the many quality horses in Whitney's stable, which Whitney had inherited at the passing of his father, W.C. Whitney, in 1904.

It appeared that Rothstein's Sporting Blood had little chance to compete with a powerful and proven runner like Prudery. But unknown to anyone outside of Rothstein's circle, Sporting Blood had been working very fast. Max Hirsch, who listed his horses as trained by "Willie Booth" in programs to distance himself from Rothstein and his reputation, had Sporting Blood in the best condition of his racing career. Hirsch told Rothstein that his training had improved Sporting Blood by as many as four or five lengths over past races.

Hirsch also told Rothstein that while Sporting Blood's improvements were probably not enough to beat a Prudery in top shape, the colt was peaking at exactly the right time, and it might just be enough to beat an off-form Prudery. Hirsch told Rothstein that Sporting Blood would be a good bet to win. With Sporting Blood's great condition and Hirsch's recommendation, Rothstein believed he had a chance to pull off an upset and make a killing on the side.

Though Whitney had the better horse, his chances of winning the Travers that year were diminished significantly, when on the day before the Travers, one of Rothstein's agents brought some important news to Rothstein — Prudery was "off her feed."[xiii]

Before Rothstein could act on the tip, he needed more information. So he called in a few favors. At that time Rothstein was paying $40,000 for a gambling pool funded by all the bookmakers in Saratoga but one that Rothstein controlled for protection. His stake in the pool influenced those who ran the town and caused hundreds of Saratoga citizens to curry his favor.

Rothstein banked on those good feelings when he paid a stableman $10 for the information that Prudery had not been worked for the race. Rothstein then discovered from a veterinarian who had examined Prudery recently, and who worked for both Whitney and Rothstein, that she was disturbed but had nothing seriously wrong with her. The vet also said that there was a chance that Prudery might come around by post time, but felt that the filly would probably not be at her best.

Even though Whitney knew that Prudery was not in top form, he decided not to pull her from the race. He didn't want the race to be a walkover for Rothstein's horse because it would have been the first time ever for the Travers. He also believed that Prudery could beat Sporting Blood even if she were not in the best of shape.

On the morning of the Travers, August 20, Rothstein was informed Prudery had shown little or no improvement. The morning line on the race had Prudery at 1-4 and Sporting Blood at 5-2. When Whitney refused to withdraw Prudery and the information of her illness did not become common knowledge, Rothstein asked a favor of Hildreth.

Unbeknownst to Whitney, the bookmakers at the track, and the fans, Hildreth and Rothstein had decided to work together again as they had four years earlier in Baltimore.

With just days before the Travers, Rothstein asked Hildreth to help divert attention away from Sporting Blood and to maximize his potential profit if Sporting Blood should manage to pull off the upset. Rothstein asked Hildreth to enter Grey Lag, one of the stars in Hildreth's barn, in the Travers.

Owned by Sinclair, Grey Lag had already beaten Sporting Blood by three lengths in the Belmont earlier that year. Grey Lag's entry in the race drastically changed the race dynamics, with many racing fans and insiders believing that Sporting Blood would now be relegated to third place as Grey Lag and Prudery fought each other for the winner's circle.

Meanwhile, Rothstein, through his agents, began to place bets on Sporting Blood with bookmakers across the country. Just before the race Rothstein bet $150,000 on Sporting Blood with handbook operators (individual street bookmakers) around the country at an average price of 3-1.

Bookmakers were only too happy to take this bet because they considered it easy money. The common belief was that Rothstein had erred significantly because Sporting Blood was not in the same class as Prudery or Grey Lag. In fact, the bookies believed the bet to be so foolish they didn't even bother to wire the money to Saratoga to be wagered at the track, so Rothstein's money didn't influence the odds. Then Rothstein placed another bet of $100,000 with the racetrack bookmakers on Sporting Blood.

At the deadline to pull an entry, thirty minutes before the race, Hildreth told the stewards that Grey Lag was, in fact, not going to run in the Travers. Grey Lag's last-minute withdrawal

The 1921 Travers with Sporting Blood over Prudery

confused and stunned the bookmakers and gamblers, leaving many to change their wagers hurriedly. With Grey Lag out, bookmakers and gamblers threw their money at Prudery, and her odds dropped to 2-7 while the odds on Sporting Blood varied from more than 2-1 to more than 3-1.[xiv]

Despite the two-horse field and some threatening clouds, a large crowd of 25,000 gathered for the Travers. Trains carrying eager fans had begun arriving the day before, and cars filled with more fans streamed into town from every direction throughout the morning. The huge crowd filled the grandstand, clubhouse, boxes, field stand, and lawns.

In the afternoon, dark clouds scattered, leaving the track dry and fast. As the race approached, the majority opinion was that Prudery was obviously the better horse and would win in a canter. Despite the short odds, large sums of money were wagered on Prudery.

But at trackside some of the trainers and "keen horsemen"[xv] observed that Prudery "seemed indisposed"[xvi] and commented that their money would follow Sporting Blood.

When the horses gathered at the post, Laverne Fator rode Prudery, who carried 121 pounds to the post, while Lawrence Lyke was up on Sporting Blood, who carried 115 pounds.

The race developed exactly as Rothstein had hoped. Both horses had a good start with Sporting Blood taking the lead, but Prudery stayed close. As they made the clubhouse turn, Prudery moved in front of Sporting Blood and kept her lead through the backstretch.

Despite the heavy odds, Prudery never managed to pull away and Sporting Blood remained close, never more than a length behind. As the two horses entered the far turn, a general sense of dread swept through the stands and the betting ring as the crowd realized that Prudery was not going to be able to pull away from the underdog. Coming out of the turn, Lyke first brought Sporting Blood up to Prudery's withers and then passed her.

Down the stretch Sporting Blood was ahead by a neck, but at the mile mark Prudery's lack of conditioning began to show. When Fator asked Prudery to make her move, she couldn't respond. Prudery faltered, fell off stride, and floundered badly as Sporting Blood passed her. Fator continued to ask for more from Prudery, and even used his whip. But the race was over when Prudery pinned her ears and sulked.

Cries of disbelief, "Prudery's beaten,"[xvii] ran through the stunned crowd, and exasperated gamblers and bookmakers watched as Lyke turned back and looked over his shoulders at Prudery at the finish line. Sporting Blood won by two lengths in 2:05 4/5. For his troubles Arnold Rothstein won the Travers purse of $10,725, plus $450,000 in bets from bookmakers across the country. After the race his friend Sam Hildreth received a cut.

Rothstein's plan to create a diversion moments before the race had succeeded in confusing the bookies and gamblers in the Travers, and allowed Rothstein to profit handsomely. But it was not the first time Rothstein had confused the bookies and gamblers with last-minute manipulations.

On August 27, 1920, Rothstein decided the conditions were right for him to win $1 million on a single race at Saratoga. Rothstein had in his stable a two-year-old maiden colt, meaning he was winless, entered in a five-furlong selling race with no really outstanding competition in a field of ten.

Rothstein felt Sailing B. could win, but it was the colt's first start, so no one really knew what to expect. Sailing B. opened at 30-1. As the race approached, the odds adjusted to 8-1, but moments before the race the odds slid to 4 1/2-1.

Savoring the odds, Rothstein called agents around the country with instructions to bet heavily on Sailing B. just two minutes before post time. If premature betting didn't drive down the odds, Rothstein knew he could make as much as $1.5 million.

Rothstein's scheme played out. Sailing B. jumped out from the barrier and into a long lead. Rancocas, ridden by Earl Sande, was in second all the way and finished two lengths behind Sailing B.

As it turned out, it was Sailing B.'s first and last race for Rothstein. After the race the colt was claimed for $9,000, although he "ran as though he was worth much more."[xviii]

The $9,000 Rothstein won, however, was insignificant when compared with his gambling coup. He won somewhere between $850,000 and $950,000,[xix] but it still wasn't enough, and Rothstein wanted to know why. Later he learned that one of his agents had placed a $1,500 bet on Sailing B. twenty minutes before the race instead of two minutes before because the agent's watch ran fast.

As his successes and profits continued to pile up, rumors spread that Rothstein, like Walbaum almost forty years earlier, fixed the races. One day August Belmont II confronted Rothstein, accusing him of being a bad influence on the sport. "You know what people are saying, Arnold, and what they're thinking," Belmont said. "Half the country believes you were the man who fixed the World Series."[xx]

Voters in Saratoga removed officeholders friendly with gamblers and bookmakers and replaced them with candidates who had promised to clean up Saratoga's image. Rothstein then decided it was time to move back to New York City, telling his wife, "I don't like Saratoga. It's too hot."[xxi] Rothstein also put his interest in the Brook up for sale, eventually selling his share to Nat Evans.

Saratoga prospered, even after the Roaring Twenties, and the Turf society and the wealthy continued to summer there. Some of the big names who visited Saratoga included Marshall Field, John Hay Whitney, John Sanford, and Samuel D. Riddle, who were not afraid to bet large amounts in order to win even more.

In those days life was good for the Turf crowd, but not so for Arnold Rothstein. In September 1928, he had joined a high-stakes poker game and lost more than $300,000. Rothstein never liked to lose and absolutely hated paying up. He put the other gamblers off until the night of November 4 when he was called by the host of the game, George "Hump" McManus, and summoned to the Park Central Hotel. As he was readying to leave, Rothstein pulled a gun out of his pocket, gave it to an associate, and said, "Keep this for me, I will be right back."[xxii]

Soon after Rothstein entered Room 349, he was shot in the lower abdomen. He stumbled out of the room, down the service stairs, and to the street holding his stomach and asking for a cab to go home. He was taken to Polyclinic Hospital, where he died two days later.

Like Gottfried Walbaum's, Arnold Rothstein's activities cast a pall over Saratoga. Just when it appeared that racing at Saratoga couldn't sink any lower, a ray of hope appeared, not just for Saratoga, but for racing in America in general. That hope resided in the form of a big-boned and long-legged colt that seemed at first glance to be a better fit as a steeplechase jumper, rather than as a Thoroughbred racehorse.

CHAPTER 11

Man o' War

By the time Man o' War arrived in Saratoga for the 1919 meet, the two-year-old colt was already a burgeoning superstar, having won his first five starts. His owner, Samuel Riddle, a wealthy textile industrialist from Pennsylvania, had brought his stable to Saratoga because he and his wife liked it there. They kept a house on Union Avenue that became a gathering place for Turf society. Racing Man o' War at Saratoga also afforded Riddle the opportunity to show off his big red colt against the best juveniles in the country because the track featured three of the most significant races for two-year-olds: the United States Hotel Stakes, the Hopeful, and the Grand Union Hotel Stakes.

He also would be showing off his colt to those naysayers who had said a year earlier that Man o' War was not much of a racing prospect.

That August day in 1918, Riddle had been forced to spend a little more than he had hoped when unexpected competition arose in the bidding for the big chestnut colt in the Saratoga sale ring. As a result, Riddle bought Man o' War for $5,000, almost twice the sale average.

Even at that price many thought it was too much and considered the leggy, high-headed youngster whose powerful

From left, Johnny Loftus, Sam Riddle, and Louis Feustel

frame shaded a lot of ground as a colt who perhaps had potential as a steeplechase prospect.

Born shortly before midnight on March 29, 1917, Man o' War was by Fair Play, a golden chestnut sired by 1896 Belmont Stakes winner Hastings. His dam was Mahubah, a mare with good bloodlines — being by English Triple Crown winner Rock Sand — but a less than stellar race record, having only won one race.

In 1918, with the country embroiled in World War I, the colt's breeder, August Belmont II, had offered his services to the U.S. Army, been commissioned as a major, and was sent to Europe. As Belmont would not be there for his horses' training and development, he decided to put his yearlings up for sale.

At the same time, Riddle was seeking horses to add to his racing string and sent his trainers Louis Feustel and Mike Daly to inspect the yearlings Belmont had put up for sale. Belmont had offered to sell all twenty-one yearlings at a private sale for $42,000, an average of $2,000 each. Feustel and Daly inspected the yearlings and were not particularly interested. They decided that most of the yearlings were undersized and wondered whether the trip had been a waste of time.

Riddle had declined Belmont's offer at that time but then asked Feustel and Daly to inspect the yearlings again at the upcoming Saratoga sale. Neither man knew that Belmont had held one of the yearlings back from that first inspection: a big, strong, and fast red horse that Belmont's wife, Eleanor Robson Belmont, had named Man o' War to honor her husband. At the last minute Belmont had cabled from Paris to include Man o' War in the Powers-Hunter Company auction. The Belmont yearlings arrived at Saratoga just days before the August 17 sale.

This time Riddle accompanied Feustel and Daly. Again they found nothing special until they reached the very last stall, and in the shadows stood a big red yearling with a commanding presence. Riddle asked the trainers to lead the colt out where he could see him and later recalled, "He simply bowled me over."[i]

Riddle was not alone in his enthusiasm for this son of Mahubah. Feustel had been wanting to train a Fair Play colt and admired Man o' War's dam, whom he had trained.[ii] With Feustel's encouragement, Riddle went to the auction determined to buy Belmont's big red yearling. That year the sale averaged $2,474, and the highest-priced colt, Golden Broom, sold for $15,600. A blaze-faced chestnut, the sale topper had been purchased by Riddle's niece by marriage, Mrs. Walter M. Jeffords.[iii]

Riddle actually had decided to buy two colts that day, Gun Muzzle and Man o' War, and hoped he could purchase Man o' War for about $2,500. As impressive as the chestnut was, he was a gangly colt whose dam had only won $700 in her racing career. Robert L. Gerry, Riddle's most persistent competitor in the bidding for Man o' War, considered the colt a good steeplechase prospect while others at the sale considered Man o' War much too big and awkward to become a strong runner.[iv]

After acquiring Man o' War, Riddle decided to keep him at Saratoga to be broken and trained, and that same afternoon a jockey was lifted onto a saddle on the colt's back, resulting in a wild scene that Riddle never forgot.[v] He recalled, "He fought like a tiger. He screamed with rage and fought us so hard that it took several days before he could be handled with safety."[vi]

Man o' War as a yearling

Like his father, Fair Play, who was known to try to bite horses attempting to pass him, Man o' War was a strong-willed horse with a mind of his own. Feustel managed to get Man o' War saddled that afternoon but not without a huge struggle. As soon as a jockey mounted, Man o' War bucked and sent him flying. Man o' War then pranced and bucked around the paddock for fifteen minutes as Feustel and his helpers attempted to calm the colt.[vii]

Feustel described the arduous and risky process by which they finally broke Man o' War to saddle, "You had to tighten his girth a little bit, let him walk around, then tighten it another hold, and let him walk around. You couldn't tighten the girth all right away or he'd jump right up and out of the stall."[viii]

Feustel, who had worked with Man o' War's grandsire Hastings for August Belmont II, was shrewd enough to realize that patience was the key. Man o' War's handlers finally won him over because the big chestnut was smart enough to realize that he couldn't resist forever. But Riddle said, "I don't think we saddled him once during his races ... that he didn't show by his actions that he remembered his breaking."[ix]

After leaving Saratoga, Man o' War joined the rest of Riddle's horses at the owner's farm near Berlin, Maryland, to receive his early schooling.

Feustel's and Riddle's patience with the tempestuous colt was eventually rewarded, though Feustel and his stable foreman, George Conway, treated Man o' War no differently than they did the other colts. He was ridden each day to acclimate him to the reins, then walked, rubbed, washed, and put back in the stall. Sometimes the chestnut colt was allowed to sprint under wraps for an eighth or a quarter of a mile, and soon Man o' War showed the long, powerful stride that made him the most promising yearling on the farm.

At first Man o' War had not been regarded with any special recognition on the farm and was known as "Mahubah's colt,"[x] but as he continued to grow and show his great potential, the stablehands fondly called him "Big Red."[xi]

Close to the Riddle farm, where Big Red was being trained, was the farm of Mr. and Mrs. Walter M. Jeffords, and the two farms shared a training track. Each year the two stables matched their most promising young horses against each other. The Jeffordses and their handlers were confident that their expensive colt Golden Broom would easily defeat the awkward Riddle colt, and a date to test the two was set in the fall of 1918. When Man o' War met Golden Broom in trials on that track, it turned out that the Jeffordses were right. Because Man o' War had such a long stride, he struggled to make a good start. The Jeffords colt's fast start won the race while Man o' War only slowly reached his stride.

Over the winter months Man o' War stayed at the Maryland farm for training. During training and racing, some racehorses become finicky eaters but not Man o' War. He loved to eat and continued to grow. While few three-year-olds ever weigh more than 1,050 pounds, by the time the two-year-old Man o' War debuted on June 6, 1919, he weighed almost one thousand pounds.

The training pony on the farm, a big brown hunter named Major Treat, usually led the Thoroughbreds from the stable to the track, and once at the track Man o' War was always eager to run.[xii] While Man o' War clearly enjoyed showing his speed, he continued to present some problems for his handlers. In his stall Man o' War could be gentle as a lamb, but once he was taken from his stall, the willful colt was a handful.

Early in the 1919 season Man o' War was taken to Pimlico for his first lesson in leaving the barrier. He continued to have trouble with his legs, but once he reached his stride, usually by the quarter-mile mark, he easily passed the other colts.

Johnny Loftus, a talented and experienced jockey, was working for Riddle at the time and carefully watched the colt's progress.

Loftus had grown up in Chicago. He began riding professionally at the age of fourteen and would go on to a very successful career that spanned from 1909 to 1919, winning 580 of 2,449 races, a 23.7 percent success rate.[xiii] He was known to possess an excellent sense of pace, had won the 1918 Preakness on War Cloud, and in the spring of 1919 rode Sir Barton to win the first Triple Crown.

One morning Loftus was brought in to replace Man o' War's regular exercise rider, Clyde Gordon. The ride was smooth until Man o' War broke out of a jog. Suddenly, the deep-chested colt reared, until he was almost completely upright. Man o' War then jumped at least five feet in the air, jumped twice more, and ran a blazing half-mile in forty-seven seconds, which was only slightly off the then-world record of :46 1/5.[xiv]

Loftus allegedly was so stunned by the incident that he was

white and shaking when he returned to the stable.[xv] However, the incident didn't prevent Loftus from becoming Man o' War's regular rider — fortunate for everyone involved.

As the spring progressed, Man o' War's workouts grew progressively harder and faster. He was so eager to run that the exercise boys only had to get in the saddle and hang on.

The high-strung Man o' War continued to fight the barriers that were used to start races. Probably sensing greatness in the colt, Loftus befriended Man o' War and regularly visited his new mount on non-racing days. He started working with Man o' War and helped the colt leave the barrier and hit his stride fast. To overcome Man o' War's early problems with starts, Loftus became expert at slightly agitating the colt just before races so that Man o' War tended to forget about any shenanigans and become more focused and capable of making a strong start. The colt listened to Loftus, grew eager, if not impetuous, about starting, and would act up if the starts were delayed.

Man o' War opened his racing career with a six-length maiden score at Belmont and three days later won the five-and-a-half-furlong Keene Memorial by three lengths in the mud in a time of 1:05 3/5.[xvi] With Loftus up, Man o' War won his first five starts and was given some time to rest.

Then it was time for the Saratoga meet.

Man o' War arrived at Horse Haven — the old trotting track where the original 1863 race meeting was held, located right across from the present-day track — in July. Man o' War immediately took to the clean air, warm days, and cool nights.

The competition among the two-year-olds promised to be intense and included Harry Payne Whitney's Upset and Wildair, as well as the horse that Whitney's trainer James Rowe thought to be the best in their stable, John P. Grier.

There were, however, other quality juveniles at the meeting: Rouleau, sired by Tracery; Carmandale; David Harum;

Donnacona; and the Jeffordses' colt, Golden Broom. The meeting also drew the filly Bonnie Mary, who had some impressive wins of her own including the Fashion, the Juvenile, and the Great American Stakes. In the Great American Stakes, Bonnie Mary had beaten two quality horses, On Watch and Upset, and had broken a track record by a full second.

Man o' War made his Saratoga debut in the six-furlong United States Hotel Stakes on August 2. He was heavily favored at 9-10 even though he carried 130 pounds. Other horses in the field of ten included Upset, at 6-1; Bonnie Mary at 9-2; Carmandale, 25-1; and Homely, also at 25-1.

Man o' War was slotted in the eighth post position while Upset was on the rail with Bonnie Mary next to him. The race was almost over as soon as it started. When the barrier flew up, Man o' War bolted away and grabbed a commanding lead. Laverne Fator attempted to drive Carmandale to stay with Man o' War, but after two furlongs Carmandale could not sustain the pace. In the homestretch, Upset, Homely, and Bonnie Mary made a run and generated some excitement in the crowd. But the runner-up, Upset, could not get within two lengths of Man o' War, who finished in 1:12 2/5.

After his string of early season victories, there was much talk about Man o' War as a potential superstar deserving mention in the same breath with New York Yankee baseball great Babe Ruth. As Man o' War headed for the three-quarters-mile Sanford Memorial at Saratoga, on August 13, the Riddle camp brimmed with confidence, and Mrs. Riddle even planned a pre-race party with a cake featuring Man o' War's name in frosting.

Man o' War was scheduled to face quality competition in the Sanford, including Golden Broom, who had recently won the Saratoga Special, in which he defeated the good Whitney colt Wildair. The Jeffords colt possessed an efficient running style that gave him a competitive advantage as he ran closer to the ground with a smooth rhythm. Just days before the Sanford, Man o' War and Golden Broom had worked together in a private match of three furlongs, a trial in which Man o' War was forced to push himself, and had run each furlong in' eleven seconds, only beating Golden Broom by a length.

One of the largest crowds of the meeting, about 20,000 people, gathered for the Sanford. The seven-horse field included the imported filly Donnacona at 30-1 with Kelsay up; Armistice at 100-1 with McAtee in the saddle; Captain Alcock, a 100-1 longshot, ridden by Robinson; The Swimmer at 50-1 with Simpson in the saddle; Upset at 8-1 ridden by Willie Knapp; and Golden Broom at 2-1, with Eddie Ambrose in the saddle.

Both Man o' War and Golden Broom carried 130 pounds while Upset and The Swimmer carried only 115. The other horses carried 112 pounds,

Trouble started even before the race when Golden Broom, who gave every indication of being a "very shy and green colt,"[xvii] had to be led from the paddock, past the stands, and up to the starting post, by a pony. As soon as he arrived at the post, the nervous Golden Broom began acting up.

It was unfortunate that Mars Cassidy, the regular starter, was sick. One of the placing judges, and a former starter, the aging Charlie Pettingill, was forced to replace him. While Pettingill had been known as a competent starter, he had had trouble all day and there had been only two good starts out of the seven races that day.

Acting up more than usual, Man o' War soon joined Golden Broom in his antics. Golden Broom actually broke through the barrier three times, and Upset, who was placed near Golden Broom, also tried to break through the tape at the line.

After several minutes the field finally appeared to have settled, but only the horses near the rail were ready. Just before the start, Man o' War appeared to have calmed down but was actually on

Upset holding off Man o' War in the Sanford

his toes.[xviii]

When Pettingill finally got the field away, Man o' War was turned sideways and forced "to get set after the others were under way."[xix]

Meanwhile, Upset took the lead, but Golden Broom, on the rail, passed him and at the half-mile mark led by a head. Donnacona was third. Golden Broom was setting a terrific pace, and Man o' War had passed only one horse in the first half-mile.

When Man o' War finally reached full stride, he flashed the brilliant speed that made him such a great horse. Along the backstretch he passed Armistice and The Swimmer and moved into fourth place. Then Loftus moved Man o' War to the railing where he was boxed in by the failing Donnacona. When Donnacona "gave up the chase,"[xx] the undefeated favorite moved into third.

In the homestretch Man o' War was only two lengths behind Upset and Golden Broom. In front of Man o' War, Knapp refused to allow Upset to pass the fading Golden Broom because he feared creating a path for Man o' War, who was moving up. Later he said, "If I'd given so much as an inch, the race would've been as good as over ..."[xxi]

Golden Broom's lead was fading. When he suddenly gave up after a few strides down the stretch, Upset raced past him, followed by Man o' War. At that point, Knapp urged Upset to make his move. "I gunned Upset with my bat [whip] and galloped to the top in a pair of jumps," said Knapp.[xxii]

Despite the horrible start and having to come from behind, Man o' War was just three-quarters of a length behind Upset with a hundred feet to the wire. Man o' War charged for the finish, and at the wire he had pulled within a neck of the leader. Given another twenty feet, he would have passed the Whitney colt, but Upset hung on to the lead and won the six-furlong race in 1:11 1/5. Golden Broom placed third, followed by Captain Alcock, Armistice, The Swimmer, and Donnacona.

It was a shocking upset, and later there would be accusations of improper behavior on the part of Knapp and Loftus, both of whom had their licenses denied the following year. But the prevailing attitude at the track that day was that Man o' War had not been discredited. While he had not been able to pass Upset at the wire, "he stood out as the best horse in the race by a large margin"[xxiii] because he had gamely fought back from "the very worst of the racing luck"[xxiv] and almost had caught a good horse that carried fifteen pounds less and that "had a start of three to four lengths on him."[xxv]

It was the only loss Man o' War ever suffered, and stable employees swore he had nightmares for weeks. Amidst the gloom pervading the Man o' War camp, a lot of speculation centered on how Man o' War would handle his first defeat. But ten days after the Sanford, Man o' War showed up at the starting barrier, confident and ready to resume his winning ways.

Man o' War faced nine opponents for the six-furlong Grand

Union Hotel Stakes, including Upset, who, with Knapp up again, was at 7-1; and Blazes, who was 8-1. The betting public remained confident in Man o' War, making him the odds-on favorite at 1-2.

While there had been heavy criticism of Loftus for his ride in the Sanford, he remained on Man o' War. The start was clean. There were no mistakes in this race, and the track was fast. After two furlongs Man o' War had a decisive lead with Upset staying close, and Blazes in third. Man o' War was never seriously challenged after he took the lead as Loftus vainly attempted to rein in his horse in the last eighth of a mile. Man o' War won easily in 1:12, followed by Upset and Blazes.

On an oppressively hot and humid closing day, August 30, Saratoga featured one of the big events of the meeting, the three-quarters-mile Hopeful Stakes for two-year-olds. Man o' War was, of course, the odds-on favorite, and nemesis Upset was back for another try, this time with stablemate Dr. Clark in the mix. Other contenders in the eight-horse field included the good fillies Constancy, at 10-1, and Cleopatra, at 8-1.

Constancy, who had just won the Spinaway Stakes, was known to be a fast breaker with good speed. She was owned by Commander J.K.L. Ross, who had campaigned a three-year-old that would be known to history as the winner of the first Triple Crown, Sir Barton. Cleopatra, owned by W.R. Coe and bred by A.B. Hancock, would win the Champagne Stakes.

For the Hopeful, Whitney's trainer, James Rowe, had devised a detailed strategy for beating Man o' War. Dr. Clark was to set an early fast pace in hopes of tiring out Big Red and then run interference for Upset. This plan would allow Upset to stay close enough so he could catch Man o' War at the finish.

Just as the horses reached the post, a severe thunderstorm drenched Saratoga and turned the track into a quagmire. The stinging rain was so heavy it temporarily blinded the horses.

Adding to the chaos, other horses appeared to crowd Man o' War as the rival jockeys were determined to get a good break while preventing Man o' War from any advantage. Loftus was forced to pull Man o' War from the barrier to straighten him out on several occasions, but as soon as they returned to the barrier, another jockey would pull his horse from the line.

As the turmoil continued, Man o' War became agitated and kicked out at the other horses several times, actually landing a blow on Ethel Gray, the number seven horse. The horses continued to act up and several horses, including Man o' War, broke from the barrier. It was all Loftus could do to restrain his colt from "running away on one occasion."[xxvi] When starter Mars Cassidy finally organized the horses in a good start, twelve minutes had passed, and many observers wondered whether Cassidy had lost control.

At the break Constancy jumped into the lead with Dr. Clark beside her. After an eighth of a mile, she was ahead by two lengths. Dr. Clark was second, and following Rowe's plan, attempted to push the pace and tire the rest of the field. He was followed by Captain Alcock and Man o' War.

As the field headed into the homestretch, Man o' War passed Captain Alcock and Dr. Clark, but Constancy maintained a lead until they came out of the turn, with Man o' War so close he almost stumbled over her.[xxvii]

Unfazed by the muddy track, Man o' War passed Constancy in two or three long strides. He was pulling away so easily and rapidly that Loftus pulled him up and peeked back under his arm to see if any other horses were near. The closest horse was Cleopatra, who had overtaken Constancy in the stretch.

Man o' War's rival, Upset, had broken well and stayed close through the backstretch. Though Upset valiantly tried to keep up, he never contended. The early pace had drained him and the fading Dr. Clark. In the slop, Man o' War won by four lengths in

1:13, followed by Cleopatra and Constancy.

Man o' War's last race of the season was at Belmont Park in the six-furlong Futurity Stakes on September 13. It marked his first encounter with John P. Grier. The race, however, was a repeat of Man o' War's other victories. The big chestnut won easily in 1:11 3/5. John P. Grier was a solid second.

At the end of the 1919 season, Man o' War led all other two-year-olds with $83,325 in earnings. The big red colt's appearance regularly drew huge crowds. A true superstar, Man o' War was acclaimed in the press and adored by the public.

He was then sent to winter quarters and exercised his tremendous appetite, eating twelve quarts of oats daily, about three quarts more than the average racehorse. His eating habits were so greedy that Feustel actually had to put a bit in his mouth to keep Man o' War from bolting his food.

By April 1920 the once gangly yearling had become a powerful three-year-old. Man o' War weighed 1,125 pounds, stood 16.2 hands tall, and ran with a stride of twenty-five to twenty-eight feet.[xxviii] The plum races for three-year-olds lay ahead, ripe for

Man o' War besting John P. Grier in the Dwyer

the picking.

Man o' War began the 1920 season without his regular jockey as the independent-minded Loftus had had his license suspended at the end of the 1919 season. Clarence Kummer, who had posted a very successful 1919 season and would go on to be the leading money winner of 1920, was hired to replace him.

Man o' War's first start was in the Preakness. Unfortunately, at this time, Riddle didn't believe three-year-old horses were physically prepared to run more than a mile early in the season; therefore, his star was not allowed to compete in the Kentucky Derby, probably denying history a second consecutive Triple Crown winner after Sir Barton.

Man o' War won the Preakness easily. From there, he added victories in the Withers Stakes, Belmont Stakes, and the Stuyvesant Handicap.

It was not until the one-and-one-eighth-mile Dwyer Stakes, on July 10, that he was challenged by the darling of the Rowe barn, John P. Grier — Man o' War's only opponent for the race.

John P. Grier, a compact and powerful chestnut sired by Whisk Broom II, and named after a prominent financier, was one of the fastest horses over a mile that Rowe had ever clocked. In fact, the previous year Rowe had considered the speedy colt to be his best hope in his all-consuming quest to defeat Man o' War, but circumstance and Upset had gotten the job done instead. As John P. Grier was only carrying 108 pounds to Man o' War's 126, the time was ripe for Rowe to pull off another defeat of the great horse.

Man o' War maintained a slight lead at the start, but the two three-year-olds ran a tight race, and neither of the horses was able to pull away. They covered the first quarter-mile in :23 2/5, the half-mile in :46, and six furlongs in 1:09 3/5.

The two colts continued the torrid pace, and the time for the mile was 1:35 4/5, equaling the world record. Kummer even lashed Man o' War with the whip, but he just couldn't shake the persistent John P. Grier. John P. Grier pulled even and actually moved ahead momentarily. As the horses traded slight leads, the crowd roared its approval. Man o' War seemed to have finally met his match, but with just a sixteenth of a mile left, John P. Grier faltered. Jockey Eddie Ambrose knew his horse had given all he could and let up. Man o' War pulled away to win by a length and a half in 1:49 2/5, a new American record for nine furlongs. After the race Clarence Kummer said it was one of his best races with Man o' War.

Man o' War returned to Saratoga for the one-and-three-sixteenths-mile Miller Stakes on August 7. He was without Clarence Kummer, who had fractured his shoulder riding another horse. Instead, the young but gifted Earl Sande was aboard. Man o' War faced only two opponents — Donnacona and King Albert — and was the prohibitive favorite. Donnacona gamely chased Man o' War for three-quarters of a mile but then faltered as Man o' War drew away to win by six lengths. Sande visibly tried to hold back his horse at the end.

Man o' War had appeared to lope cheerfully around the track, but in actuality had come within three-fifths of a second of the track record at 1:56 3/5. After the race an exhausted Sande said, "I never felt anything under me like that colt in my life. Why, he is the greatest horse I've ever ridden."[xxix]

Two weeks later, on August 21, Man o' War lined up for the mile and a quarter Travers Stakes. This time James Rowe, who had become thoroughly obsessed with defeating Man o' War, was confident victory was in hand. Rowe boasted, "Now, I've got him"[xxx] and threw the double-barreled entry of Upset and John P. Grier into the fray. Many racing pundits agreed and believed that the only real chance to catch Man o' War that season would be with these two fine horses. Upset had defeated Man o' War in

1919, and John P. Grier had tested him thoroughly earlier that summer. In addition, both horses had been rested for a month.

Part of Rowe's confidence, no doubt, stemmed from Sande's unavailability to ride in the Travers. Man o' War had clearly been very happy with his newest jockey, but Sande had committed to ride for Commander J.K.L. Ross in Canada. To replace Sande, Riddle employed Andy Schuttinger to ride Man o' War. Schuttinger was considered by his peers to be an excellent judge of pace, but he was Man o' War's fourth jockey in two seasons and his third consecutive rider in three starts.

His two quality opponents notwithstanding, Man o' War was favored at 2-9, while both Upset and John P. Grier were listed at 18-5.

Even Man o' War's owner had not been sure of victory. After the race Riddle confided, "I will own that this was the only time I was ever nervous, really nervous, about the outcome of a race that Man o' War went into after he had shown up what he was … But I knew he had the two best three-year-olds, aside from himself, to beat … I had watched them in their training and knew they were both as fit as the man called the greatest living trainer could make them."[xxxi]

The eagerly anticipated race drew the largest crowd ever at Saratoga, at that time. The stands were full, and the crowd stretched for a quarter of a mile along the rail in a packed mass that extended back to the stands.[xxxii] The crowd was growing so large that the infield was made available to the public. Five thousand fans gathered there to watch the race. All had come to see Man o' War meet the only two three-year-olds that had any chance to beat him.

As Man o' War would be burdened with 129 pounds while Upset would carry 123 pounds, and John P. Grier, 115, there was much speculation as to whether the champion would meet his match this time. Some in the crowd believed that Man o' War

Man o' War winning the Travers, again over John P. Grier

was in for the battle of his life, and that John P. Grier would be better prepared; others whispered that "Man o' War had had too many fast trials and that he was probably stepping to his doom today."xxxiii

Buoyed with confidence, Rowe strategized a way to defeat his nemesis. The trainer knew John P. Grier could not beat Man o' War by himself and told Ambrose to take him to the lead and do the mile in no greater than 1:35, with the intention of tiring Big Red. Rowe's plan was that when John P. Grier exhausted himself, Upset would take control of the race and pass both John P. Grier and Man o' War. Rowe believed he had a chance because Upset preferred the mile and a quarter distance of the Travers and liked coming from behind to overtake tiring horses.

Riddle had his own strategy. To ensure that Man o' War would not be overextended by John P. Grier and then passed at the finish by a surging Upset, he told Schuttinger, "Take him out in front the minute the flag falls. Keep him going. Don't let either of them get near you. Just show them up if anyone thinks that they can beat him. That's all. He will do the rest."[xxxiv]

Man o' War was first to reach the starting post.

The crowd, anticipating a great race, saw one. John P. Grier jumped out from the start and attempted to set the pace while Man o' War was unusually slow breaking from the gate. With two huge strides, however, he took the lead and was a length in front before either Upset or John P. Grier was in full stride.

Schuttinger gave Man o' War rein, and the race was almost over at the first turn. Both John P. Grier and Upset struggled to gain the rail, but Man o' War was there first. When Schuttinger let Man o' War run free, he took a two-length lead over John P. Grier, with Upset following easily three lengths farther back.

The pace was extremely fast, and Ambrose tried to push John P. Grier for more speed. John P. Grier valiantly attempted to duel Man o' War for the first three-quarters of a mile, as Schuttinger tried to rein the favorite in. But his colt could never get closer than Man o' War's heels. With just a sliver of space between them at the far turn, Man o' War refused to be caught and accelerated. Ambrose tried using the whip, but John P. Grier could not keep the pace and lost ground.

Upset, with Rodriguez up, was still following the two leaders and didn't make his move until they hit the stretch. By then Ambrose knew that John P. Grier had nothing left and he let up as Upset passed him. But Upset could not make a run on Man o' War even with Schuttinger actually standing in the stirrups in an attempt to slow Man o' War down. Big Red finished in front by two and a half lengths. Upset finished second with the badly tiring John P. Grier in third.

Man o' War next won twice at Belmont, including a one-hundred-length demolition in the Lawrence Realization, then once at Havre de Grace in Maryland, before his final race, at Kenilworth Park in Canada. There had been a great public

Sam Riddle and Man o' War

demand for a meeting between Man o' War and champion Sir Barton.

Finally, a mile and a quarter race was arranged for October 12 and featured the greatest purse offered at that time, $75,000, plus a $5,000 Tiffany gold cup. Four-year-old Sir Barton, while not as consistent as Man o' War, had recently won the Saratoga Handicap, as well as the Merchants' and Citizens' Handicap while carrying 133 pounds.

Man o' War, again under Clarence Kummer, carried 120 pounds. He was the 5-100 favorite while Sir Barton, with Frank Keogh up, carried 126 pounds, and was given 555-100 odds.

When the barrier was released, Man o' War jumped into the lead and set a commanding pace. After a quarter-mile Sir Barton was not gaining. Even though Keogh used his whip, Sir Barton still couldn't gain any ground. Man o' War won by seven lengths, set a track record of 2:03, and was retired.

His lifetime record was twenty wins and one loss, he never won by less than a length, and won one race by an astounding one hundred lengths. Man o' War earned $249,465, surpassing Domino's $193,550, eclipsing a record that had stood for twenty-six years.

In twenty-three years at stud, Man o' War was almost as successful. He produced sixty-four stakes winners, including War Admiral, a Triple Crown winner and Horse of the Year.

From his retirement until just months before his death, Man o' War was visited at his Lexington, Kentucky, home by somewhere between 1.5 million to 3 million people from all over the world eager to see the legendary champion.

Even his owner was awed by the magnificent competitor he had bought one mid-summer day years ago in Saratoga. As the great champion was approaching the end, Sam Riddle said of Man o' War, "We do not know to this day how fast he was, as we were afraid to let him down. We feared he might injure himself."[xxxv]

REFERENCES

CHAPTER 1

i   *New York Times*, 2 May 1878, pp. 1-2.

ii   *New York Times*, 2 May 1878, pp. 1-2.

iii   *New York Daily Tribune*, 2 May 1878, p. 5.

iv   *Chicago Daily Tribune*, 1 Aug. 1874, p. 4.

v   Ibid.

vi   Ibid.

vii   Ibid.

viii   Ibid.

ix   *New York Times*, 2 May 1878, pp. 1-2.

x   *New York Times*, 2 May 1878, pp. 1-2.

xi   http://experts.about.com/e/j/jo/john_morrissey.htm

xii   *New York Times*, 2 May 1878, pp. 1-2.

xiii   *Chicago Daily Tribune*, 1 Aug. 1874, p. 4.

xiv   *New York Times*, 2 May 1878, pp. 1-2.

xv   *Chicago Daily Tribune*, 1 Aug. 1874, p. 4.

xvi   *Chicago Daily Tribune*, 1 Aug. 1874, p. 4.

xvii   *New York Times*, 2 May 1878, pp. 1-2.

xviii   Britten, Evelyn Barrett. *Chronicles of Saratoga*. 1959, p. 90.

xix   Hotaling, Edward. *They're Off! Horse Racing at Saratoga*. 1995, p.36.

xx   Joki, Robert. *Saratoga Lost: Images of Victorian America*. 1998, p. 134.

xxi   Manning, Landon, *The Noble Animals: Tales of the Saratoga Turf*, 1973, p. 63.

CHAPTER 2

i   Britten, *Chronicles of Saratoga*, p. 87.

ii   Manning, *The Noble Animals*, p. 61.

iii   *New York Times*, 2 May 1878, p. 1-2.

iv   Lane, Wheaton J., *Commodore Vanderbilt: An Epic of the Steam Age*, 1942, p. 109.

v   Lane, *Commodore Vanderbilt*, p. 83.

vi   Ibid.

vii   Hotaling, *They're Off!*, p. 42.

viii   Manning, *The Noble Animals*, p. 57.

ix   Leslie, Anita, *The Remarkable Mr. Jerome*, 1954, p. 86.

x   Rugoff, Milton. *America's Gilded Age: Intimate Portraits from an Era of Extravagance and Change, 1850-1890*, 1989, p. 61.

xi   Leslie, *The Remarkable Mr. Jerome*, p. 59.

xii   Manning, *The Noble Animals*, p. 58.

CHAPTER 3

i   *Wilkes' Spirit of the Times*, 11 July 1863, Vol. VIII, p. 297.

ii   *Wilkes' Spirit of the Times*, 9 July 1863, Vol. X, p. 291.

iii   Ibid.

iv   *Wilkes' Spirit of the Times*, 11 July 1863, Vol. VIII, p. 297.

v   *Wilkes' Spirit of the Times*, 11 July 1863, Vol. VIII, p. 297.

vi   Hotaling, p. 45.

vii   *Wilkes' Spirit of the Times*, 15 Aug. 1863, Vol. VIII, p. 369.

viii   *Wilkes' Spirit of the Times*, 15 Aug. 1863, Vol. VIII, p. 369.

ix   Veitch, Michael. *Foundation of Fame: Nineteenth Century Thoroughbred Racing in Saratoga Springs*. 2004. Advantage Press. New York.

x   *Wilkes' Spirit of the Times*, 12 Dec. 1863, Vol. IX, p. 233.

xi   *Wilkes' Spirit of the Times*, 15 Aug. 1863, Vol. VIII, p. 369.

xii   Hotaling, *They're Off!*, p. 44.

xiii   Ibid.

xiv   *Wilkes' Spirit of the Times*, 15 Aug. 1863, Vol. VIII, p. 369.

xv   Ibid.

xvi   Ibid.

xvii   Ibid.

xviii   Ibid.

xix   Ibid.

xx   *Wilkes' Spirit of the Times*, 9 Jan. 1864, Vol. IX, p. 301.

xxi   *Wilkes' Spirit of the Times*, 15 Aug. 1863, Vol. VIII, p. 369.

xxii   *Wilkes' Spirit of the Times*, 15 Aug. 1863, Vol. VIII, p. 370.

xxiii   Ibid.

xxiv   Ibid.

xxv   Ibid.

xxvi   Ibid.

xxvii   Hotaling, *They're Off!*, p. 47.

xxviii   Ibid., p. 49.

xxix   *Wilkes' Spirit of the Times*, 5 Sept. 1863, Vol. IX, p. 9.

xxx   Hotaling, *They're Off!*, p. 48.

xxi   *Wilkes' Spirit of the Times*, 12 Dec. 1863, Vol. IX, p. 233.

xxxii   *Wilkes' Spirit of the Times*, 19 Dec. 1863, Vol. IX, p. 254.

CHAPTER 4

i *Wilkes' Spirit of the Times*, 4 June 1864, Vol. X, p. 244.

ii Robertson, William H. P., *The History of Thoroughbred Racing in America*, 1964, p. 120.

iii www.tbheritage.com/Portraits/Norfolk.html

iv *Wilkes' Spirit of the Times*, 4 June 1864, Vol. X, p. 217.

v Ibid.

vi *Wilkes' Spirit of the Times*, 18 June 1864, Vol. X, p. 244.

vii *New York Times*, 22 June 1859, Vol. VIII, no. 2420, p. 4.

viii *New York Times*, 25 Aug. 1859, Vol. VIII, no. 2474, p. 3.

ix *Wilkes' Spirit of the Times*, 18 June 1864, Vol. X, p. 244.

x *Wilkes' Spirit of the Times*, 18 June 1864, Vol. X, p. 248.

xi Ibid.

xii *Wilkes' Spirit of the Times*, 18 June 1864, Vol. X, p. 254.

xiii Ibid.

xiv *Wilkes' Spirit of the Times*, 18 June 1864, Vol. X, p. 244.

xv *Wilkes' Spirit of the Times*, 18 June 1864, Vol. X, p. 254.

xvi *Wilkes' Spirit of the Times*, 18 June 1864, Vol. X, p. 244.

xvii Ibid.

xviii *New York Times*, 12 June 1864, Vol. XIII, p. 6.

xix www.tbheritage.com/Portraits/Norfolk.html

xx *Wilkes' Spirit of the Times*, 8 June 1864, Vol. X, p. 244.

xxi *New York Times*, 12 June 1864, Vol. XIII, p. 6.

xxii *Wilkes' Spirit of the Times*, 2 Aug. 1864, Vol. X, p. 372.

xxiii *Wilkes' Spirit of the Times*, 9 July 1864, Vol. X, p. 291.

xxiv Ibid.

xxv *Wilkes' Spirit of the Times*, 13 Aug. 1864, Vol. X, p. 372.

xxvi *Wilkes' Spirit of the Times*, 13 Aug 1864, Vol. X, p. 377.

xxvii Ibid.

xxviii *Wilkes' Spirit of the Times*, 18 June 1864, Vol. X, p. 254.

xxix Ibid.

xxx Hotaling, *They're Off!*, p. 68.

xxxi www.tbheritage.com/Portraits/Glenelg.html

CHAPTER 5

i Hotaling, *They're Off!*, p. 112.

ii *New York Times*, 30 July 1875, Vol. XXIV, no. 7448, p. 1.

iii Ibid.

iv Ibid.

v Ibid.

vi   Chicago *Tribune*, 10 July 1881, p. 10.
vii   *Wilkes' Spirit of the Times*, 17 July 1875, Vol. 89, no. 23, p. 594.
viii Chicago *Tribune*, 1 Aug. 1875, p. 15.
ix   *Wilkes' Spirit of the Times*, 17 July 1875, Vol. 89, no. 23, p. 594.
x   Chicago *Tribune*, 10 July 1881, p. 10.
xi   Ibid.
xii   Ibid.
xiii Ibid.
xiv   Ibid.
xv   *Wilkes' Spirit of the Times*, 17 July 1875, Vol. 89, no. 23, p. 594.
xvi   Ibid.
xvii Ibid.
xviii Ibid.
xix   Chicago *Tribune*, 1 Aug. 1875, p. 15.
xx   Ibid.
xxi   Ibid.
xxii Ibid.
xxiii Black, David, *The King of Fifth Avenue: The Fortunes of August Belmont*, 1981, p. 290.
xxiv Chicago *Tribune*, 1 Aug. 1875, p. 15.
xxv   Ibid.
xxvi *New York Times*, 30 July 1875, Vol. XXIV, no. 7448, p. 1.
xxvii Ibid.
xxviii Hotaling, *They're Off!*, p. 121.
xxix Bradley, Hugh, *Such Was Saratoga*, 1975, p. 174.
xxx   Hotaling, *They're Off!*, p. 122.
xxxi Ibid., p. 123.

CHAPTER 6
i   Longstreet, Stephen, *Win or Lose: A Social History of Gambling in America*, 1977, p. 64.
ii   Hotaling, *They're Off!*, p. 136.
iii   Ibid., p. 140.
iv   Waller, George, *Saratoga: Saga of an Impious Era*, 1966, p. 257.
v   Hotaling, *They're Off!*, p. 136.
vi   Ibid.
vii   www.tbheritage.com/Portraits/Hindoo.html
viii www.thoroughbredchampions.com/gallery/dukeofmagenta.htm
ix   *New York Times*, 1 Aug. 1875, Vol. XXVI, no. 8076, p. 5.
x   Ibid.
xi   Ibid.

xii www.thoroughbredchampions.com/gallery/dukeofmagenta.htm
xiii *New York Times*, 17 Aug. 1877, Vol. XXVI, no. 8090, p. 8.
xiv Ibid.
xv *New York Times*, 21 July 1878, Vol. XXVII, no. 8379, p. 2.
xvi *New York Times*, 14 Aug. 1878, Vol. XXVII, no. 8400, p. 5.
xvii www.thoroughbredchampions.com/gallery/dukeofmagenta.htm
xviii www.thoroughbredchampions.com/biographies/hindoo.htm
xix www.pedigreequery.com
xx www.tbheritage.com/TurfHallmarks/Champs/
AmChamp2yoMale.html
xxi *New York Times*, 12 Aug. 1881, Vol. XXX, no. 9338, p. 5.
xxii www.tbheritage.com/Portraits/Hindoo.html

CHAPTER 7
i Waller, *Saratoga: Saga of an Impious Era*, p. 229.
ii Hotaling, *They're Off!*, p. 137.
iii Ibid.
iv Ibid.
v Ibid., p. 138.
vi Bradley, *Such Was Saratoga*, p. 209.
vii Ibid., p. 237.
viii Ibid.
ix Hotaling, *They're Off!*, p. 146.
x *New York Times*, 18 Oct. 1887, Vol. XXXVII, p. 2.
xi *New York Times*, 23 March 1891, Vol. XL, p. ??
xii *New York Times*, 30 May 1891, Vol. XL, p. ??
xiii *New York Times*, 1 Aug. 1894, Vol. XLIII, no. 13,398, p. 6.
xiv Hotaling, *They're Off!*, p. 148.
xv Ibid., p. 148-149.
xvi Ibid., p. 146.
xvii Ibid., p. 149.
xviii *Chicago Daily Tribune*, 17 Jan. 1892, Vol. LI, p. ??
xix Hotaling, *They're Off!*, p. 146.
xx Ibid., p. 157.
xxi Bradley, *Such Was Saratoga*, p. 227.
xxii Hotaling, *They're Off!*, p. 147.
xxiii Ibid.
xxiv Ibid.
xxv Ibid.
xxvi Waller, *Saratoga: Saga of an Impious Era*, p. 232.
xxvii Hotaling, *They're Off!*, p. 147.
xxviii www.answers.com/topic/alabama-stakes
xxix www.answers.com/topic/spinaway-stakes.
xxx Hotaling, *They're Off!*, p. 148.
xxxi Ibid., p. 146.

xxxii   Ibid., p. 147.
xxxiii Bradley, *Such Was Saratoga*, p. 238.
xxxiv   Hotaling, *They're Off!*, p. 147.
xxxv   *Chicago Daily Tribune*, 13 Jan. 1894, Vol. LIII, no. 13, p. 7.
xxxvi   *Chicago Daily Tribune*, 14 Jan. 1894, Vol. LIII, no. 13, p. 3.
xxxvii Ibid.
xxxviii Ibid.
xxxix   *Chicago Daily Tribune*, 13 Jan. 1894, Vol. LIII, no. 13, p. 7.
   xl   Ibid.
   xli *Chicago Daily Tribune*, 6 May 1894, Vol. LIII, no. 126, p. 5.
   xlii Ibid.
  xliii *Chicago Daily Tribune*, 26 July 1894, Vol. LIII, no. 207, p. 11.
   xliv *Wilkes' Spirit of the Times*, 28 July 1894, Vol. 128, no. 2, p. 39.
   xlv Ibid.
   xlvi *Chicago Daily Tribune*, 26 July 1894, Vol. LIII, no. 207, p. 11.
  xlvii Ibid.
 xlviii *New York Times*, 26 July 1894, Vol. XLIII, no. 13,303, p. 3.
   xlix *New York Times*, 1 Aug. 1894, Vol. XLIII, no. 13,398, p. 6.
    l   Ibid.
    li Ibid.
    lii *New York Times*, 5 Aug. 1894, Vol. XLII, no. 13,401, p. ??
   liii *New York Times*, 8 Aug. 1894, Vol. XLIII, no. 13,404, p. 3.
    liv Ibid.
    lv *New York Times*, 16 Aug. 1894, Vol. XLIII, no. 13,411, p. 3.
    lvi Ibid.
   lvii Ibid.
  lviii Ibid.
    lix Hotaling, *They're Off!*, p. 155.

CHAPTER 8
    i   Hotaling, *They're Off!*, p. 151.
    ii Ibid.
    iii Ibid.
    iv Ibid., p. 154.
    v   Pietrusza, David, *Rothstein: The Life, Times, and Murder of the Criminal Genius Who Fixed the 1919 World Series*, 2003, p. 42.
    vi Bradley, *Such Was Saratoga*, p. 285.
    vii Hotaling, *They're Off!*, p. 141.
   viii Ibid.
    ix http://www.oldandsold.com/articles01/article921.shtml
    x   Bradley, *Such Was Saratoga*, p. 252.

xi   Ibid.
xii   www.gamblingmagazine.com/articls/40/40-13.htm
xiii Waller, *Saratoga: Saga of an Impious Era*, p. 257.
xiv   Manning, *The Noble Animals*, pp. 122-123.
xv   *New York Times*, 3 Feb. 1904, Vol. LIII, no. 16874, pp. 1-2.
xvi   *New York Times*, 3 Jan. 1913, Vol. LXII, no. 20,068, pp. 1-2.
xvii Hotaling, *They're Off!*, p. 184.
xviii http://en.wikipedia.org/wiki/Roamer
xix   http://www.tbheritage.com/Portraits/RockSand.html
xx   Hotaling, *They're Off!*, p. 174.

CHAPTER 9

i   http://sky.prohosting.com/spilletta/UTHOF/sysonby.html
ii   Hotaling, p. 184.
iii   *Chicago Daily Tribune*, 2 Aug. 1904, Vol. LXIII, no. 184, p. 6.
iv   Ibid.
v   *Thoroughbred Record*, 6 Aug. 1904, Vol. 60, no. 6, p. 84.
vi   *Chicago Daily Tribune*, 2 Aug. 1904, Vol. LXIII, no. 184, p. 6.
vii   Ibid.
viii   Ibid.
ix   *Chicago Daily Tribune*, 7 Aug. 1904, Vol. LXIII, no. 32, p. B1.
x   Ibid.
xi   Ibid.
xii   *New York Times*, 3 Jan. 1913, Vol. LXII, no. 20,068, pp. 1-2.
xiii   *Chicago Daily Tribune*, 7 Aug. 1904, Vol. LXIII, no. 32, p. B1.
xiv   http://www.tbhorsepedigree.com/library/horse/Artful.php
xv   http://www.pedigreequery.com
xvi   http://www.nyra.com/Belmont/Stakes/Champagne.html
xvii   *Chicago Daily Tribune*, 15 Oct. 1904, Vol. LXIII, no. 248, p. 6.
xviii Ibid.
xix   Ibid.
xx   *Chicago Daily Tribune*, 13 Aug. 1905, p. S-3.
xxi   Jeffers, H. Paul, *Diamond Jim Brady: Prince of the Gilded Age*, 2001, p. 3.
xxii   Ibid., pp. 2-3.
xxiii *Chicago Daily Tribune*, 13 Aug. 1905, p. S-3.
xxiv   *Daily Racing Form, Charts of American Racing: July 1, 1905-December 31, 1905*, 1906. F.H. Brunell (ed.).
xxv   *New York Times*, 13 Aug. 1905, Vol. LIV, no. 17, p. 5.
xxvi   *New York Times*, 13 Aug. 1905, Vol. LIV, no. 17, p. 5.
xxvii Ibid.
xxviii *Thoroughbred Record*, 19 Aug. 1905, Vol. 62, no. 8, p. 124.

CHAPTER 10

    i   Pietrusza, *Rothstein*, p. 16.
   ii   Ibid., p. 17.
  iii Ibid., p. 18.
  iv Ibid., p. 24.
   v Ibid., p. 195.
  vi Ibid., p. 125.
 vii Ibid., p. 126.
viii Ibid., p. 160.
  ix Katcher, Leo, *The Big Bankroll: The Life and Times of Arnold Rothstein*, 1959, p. 119.
   x Ibid., p. 105.
  xi Ibid., p. 120.
 xii Ibid., p. 121.
xiii Ibid., p. 133.
xiv Waller, *Saratoga: Saga of an Impious Era*, p. 301.
 xv *New York Times*, 21 Aug. 1921, Vol. LXX, no. 23,220, pp. 3, 5.
xvi Ibid.
xvii Ibid.
xviii Ibid.
xix Pietrusza, *Rothstein*, p. 131.
 xx www.crimelibrary.com/gangsters_outlaws/mob_bosses/rothstein/feats_9.html
xxi Pietrusza, *Rothstein*, p. 134.
xxii Ibid., p. 12.

CHAPTER 11

    i   Hotaling, *They're Off!*, p. 205.
   ii   www.bbc.co.uk/dna/h2g2/A543737
  iii Ibid.
  iv www.newyorker.com/archive/content?030804fr_archive
   v Ibid.
  vi www.bbc.co.uk/dna/h2g2/A543737
 vii www.newyorker.com/archive/content?030804fr_archive
viii www.equinenet.org/heroes/mow.html
  ix Hotaling, *They're Off!*, p. 206.
   x www.newyorker.com/archive/content?030804fr_archive
  xi Ibid.
 xii Ibid.
xiii http://en.wikipedia.org/wiki/Johnny_Loftus
xiv www.newyorker.com/archive/content?030804fr_archive
 xv Ibid.
xvi www.bbc.co.uk/dna/h2g2/A543737
xvii *New York Times*, 14 Aug. 1919, Vol. LXVIII, no. 22,481, p. 17.
xviii Ibid.

xix   Ibid.

xx   Ibid.

xxi   Cooper, Page, and Roger L. Treat, *Man o' War*, 2004, p. 46.

xxii   Ibid.

xxiii   *New York Times*, 14 Aug. 1919, Vol. LXVIII, no. 22,481, p. 17.

xxiv   Ibid.

xxv   Ibid.

xxvi   *New York Times*, 31 Aug. 1919, Vol. LXVIII, no. 22,499, p. 18.

xxvii   Ibid.

xxviii   espn.go.com/sportscentury/features/00016132.html

xxix   Cooper and Treat, *Man o' War*, p. 83.

xxx   Ibid.

xxxi   Ibid., p. 85.

xxxii   *New York Times*, 22 Aug. 1920, Vol. LXIX, no. 22,856, pp. 16-18.

xxxiii   Ibid.

xxxiv   Cooper and Treat, *Man o' War*, p. 86.

xxxv   Hotaling, *They're Off!*, p. 215.

Bibliography

Black, David. *The King of Fifth Avenue: The Fortunes of August Belmont*. 1981. Dial Press: New York.

Bradley, Hugh. *Such was Saratoga*. 1940. Doubleday, Doran and Co., Inc.: New York.

Britten, Evelyn Barrett. *Chronicles of Saratoga: A Series of Articles*. 1947. Saratogian: Saratoga Springs, New York.

Chicago Daily Tribune.

Cooper, Page, and Roger L. Treat. *Man o' War*. 2004. Westholme: Yardley, Pennsylvania.

Daily Racing Form, Charts of American Racing: July 1, 1905-December 31, 1905, 1906. F.H. Brunell (ed.).

Hotaling, Edward. *They're Off! Horse Racing at Saratoga*. 1995. Syracuse University Press: Syracuse, New York.

Jeffers, H. Paul. *Diamond Jim Brady: Prince of the Gilded Age*. 2001. John Wiley & Sons, Inc.: New York.

Joki, Robert. *Saratoga Lost: Images of Victorian America*. 1998. Black Dome Press: Hensonville, NY.

Katcher, Leo. *The Big Bankroll: The Life and Times of Arnold Rothstein*. 1959. Harper & Brothers: New York.

Lane, Wheaton J., *Commodore Vanderbilt: An Epic of the Steam Age*. 1942, Knopf: New York.

Leslie, Anita. *The Remarkable Mr. Jerome*. 1954. Holt: New York.

Longstreet, Stephen. Win or Lose: A Social History of Gambling in America. 1977. The Bobbs-Merrill Company, Inc.: New York.

Manning, Landon. *The Noble Animals: Tales of the Saratoga Turf.* 1973. Saratoga Springs, New York.

New York Daily Tribune.

New York Times.

Pietrusza, David. Rothstein: *The Life, Times, and Murder of the Criminal Genius Who Fixed the 1919 World Series.* 2003. Carroll & Graf Publishers: New York.

Robertson, William H. P. *The History of Thoroughbred Racing in America.* 1964. Prentice-Hall, Inc.: Englewood Cliffs, New Jersey.

Rugoff, Milton. *America's Gilded Age: Intimate Portraits from an Era of Extravagance and Change, 1850-1890.* 1989. Holt: New York.

Thoroughbred Record.

Veitch, Michael. *Foundation of Fame: Nineteenth Century Thoroughbred Racing in Saratoga Springs.* 2004. Advantage Press: New York.

Waller, George. *Saratoga: Saga of an Impious Era.* 1966. Prentice-Hall: Englewood Cliffs, NJ.

Wilkes' Spirit of the Times.

Photo Credits

Cover: (Front) Keeneland-Cook; Widener Collection; Barbara D. Livingston; (Back) Courtesy of the George S. Bolster Collection of the Saratoga Springs History Museum; Courtesy of the National Museum of Racing and Hall of Fame; Keeneland-Cook

Chapter 1: John Morrissey: A Vision and a Beginning
Courtesy of the George S. Bolster Collection of the Saratoga Springs History Museum: 12; Courtesy of the National Museum of Racing and Hall of Fame: 23; Barbara D. Livingston: 24

Chapter 2: Movers and Shakers
Library of Congress, Prints & Photographs Division: 28; The Blood-Horse: 30, 31, 32

Chapter 3: The First Meeting
Courtesy of the National Museum of Racing and Hall of Fame: 36; Keeneland Library: 43; Courtesy of the National Museum of Racing and Hall of Fame: 46

Chapter 4: Norfolk and Kentucky
The Blood-Horse: 52, 56

Chapter 5: Doing the Most Good
The Blood-Horse: 69, 70, 79, 82

About the AUTHOR

Jon Bartels grew up in Manitowoc, Wisconsin, and graduated from the University of Wisconsin, Madison, with degrees in history and journalism. He has always admired the graceful beauty and speed of horses and horse racing, and that interest led him to join the University of Wisconsin Hoofers Riding Club.

Bartels lives in Verona, Wisconsin, and works as a freelance writer and editor, and is a member of the Wisconsin Screenwriters Forum. His writing has appeared in newspapers and magazines, and he has placed in the top ten of the Wisconsin Screenwriters Forum national screenwriting contest and has won the University of Wisconsin Writers Institute's Poem or Page Contest.